Convention Industry Council
Industry Glossary
2016 EDITION

Executive Editor: Mariela McIlwraith, CMP, CMM, MBA

Copy Editor: Dr. B.J. Reed, CMP

Lead Reviewers: Gary Murakami, GTP, GLP, CMP; Carol Norfleet, CMP, DMCP, MBA

Reviewers: CMP Volunteers – See Full List in **Appendix C - Page 79**

Published by the Convention Industry Council

Alexandria, VA, USA | February, 2016

ISBN 978-0-692-61566-9

Printed in the United States

Convention Industry Council
Industry Glossary
2016 EDITION

Table of Contents

About the Industry Glossary:

This Glossary, which has been compiled by the Convention Industry Council APEX Standards Committee and 150 active CMP volunteers, contains over 1300 words and their definitions. This is the most comprehensive reference for the specialized terminology and acronyms used throughout the convention, meetings, events and exhibition industry. It has been developed and approved "by the industry, for the industry" to be used both as a study material for those aiming to earn the CMP certification or as a reference for industry professionals overall.

About The Convention Industry Council:

Vision: To champion the economic and social value of the global meetings, conventions and exhibitions industry.

Characteristics: CIC is a leadership forum created to connect and elevate diverse voices worldwide in the meetings and events industry. A collective resource for excellence in standards and practices through certification and accreditation, CIC fosters the growth of the ROI of face-to-face events through a collabourative focus on issues, opportunities, and communities that help influence and advance the industry.

Certifications: The foremost certification for meeting and event professionals, the CMP designation recognizes those who have proven their proficiency through a combination of education, experience and passing a rigorous exam. With more than 14,000 individuals in 51 countries and territories holding the designation since its 1985 inception, CMPs are considered the leading experts in the global meetings and events industry. The CMP Healthcare Subspecialty (CMP-HC) certification distinguishes those who have mastered the unique knowledge needed to be a successful healthcare meeting professional in addition to the exacting CMP qualifications.

Other Publications: Convention Industry Council Manual, 9th Edition – A Working Guide for Effective Meetings and Conventions; CMP Today – an eNewsletter for Certified Meeting Professionals (CMP) and Pathway – an eNewsletter for CMP candidates.

Contact

Convention Industry Council
P: 1+ (571) 527-3116
E: cichq@conventionindustry.org
www.conventionindustry.org

24-Hour Hold: A term used to describe the type of reservation made on function space within a venue (hotel, convention centre, etc.). An event organiser who has 24-hour hold on a space has exclusive use and access to that space for a period of 24-hours, usually 12:01 AM – 12:00 PM.

6-by-6 Rule: Audiovisual guidelines by which a presentation slide should contain no more than six words per line of text and no more than six lines of text.

Abstract: 1) Written summaries of speeches or papers, generally between 200-500 words. **2)** A brief statement of content.

Abstract Board: Freestanding or rolling boards, typically 4' X 8' used for attaching copies of research papers for authors to discuss with participants. See POSTER BOARD and POSTER SESSION.

Acceleration Clause: A provision sometimes used in contracts to accelerate deposit payment schedule or to demand full prepayment of master account in the event of a default or lack of credit by the purchasing organisation. May also apply in other situations, such as assignments.

Acceptance: A requirement for entering into a binding contract. If a contract proposal (offer) is made, it is accepted if the offeree signs the offer as submitted. If the offeree makes any changes to the offer before signing, it is a counter offer, not acceptance.

Accepted Practices Exchange (APEX): An initiative of the meetings, conventions and exhibitions industry managed by the Convention Industry Council (CIC). APEX develops and manages the implementation of accepted practices (voluntary standards) for the industry.

Accepted Practices Exchange / ASTM International Environmentally Sustainable Standards (APEX / ASTM Standards): A compilation of 9 separate standards related to improving the environmental and social impact of events.

Accessible: The state of being usable by people with disabilities.

Accommodation: 1) Any seat, berth, room, or service provided and/or sold to a guest, attendee or passenger. **2)** A step taken to allow a person with a disability to participate in an event.

Accreditation: Official authorization or approval to **1)** to provide with credentials; **2)** to recognize or verify act of conforming with a standard; **3)** to recognize a post-secondary institution or degree-bearing programme as satisfying and maintaining academic standards.

Accrual Accounting: 1) An accounting method that enters income and expenses into the books at the time of contract versus when payment is received or expenses incurred (cash accounting). **2)** A system in which revenue and expenses are accounted for as soon as they are committed.

Act of God: An extraordinary natural disaster such as extreme weather, flood, hurricane, tornado, earthquake, etc. that cannot be reasonably foreseen or prevented and over which a contracting party has no reasonable control. The occurence makes performance of the contract illegal, impracticable or impossible, leaving the contract parties with no legal responsibility to continue performance of the contract. See FORCE MAJEURE.

Action Station: Chefs prepare foods to order and serve them fresh to guests. Also called Performance Stations, Carving Stations, or Exhibition Cooking.

Actual Weight: Also known as gross shipping weight. Determined by **1)** weighing a vehicle empty, **2)** loading a shipment and returning the vehicle to the scale to obtain the new weight, and **3)** subtracting the empty from the loaded weight. Can also be obtained by individually weighing each piece of freight. See GROSS WEIGHT, TARE WEIGHT.

Ad Hoc Committee: Committee formed to deal with a specific issue or task; the committee is dissolved upon making its final report to the organisation that created it.

Ad Valorem Tax: Tax applied to an item according to the value of an item. See DUTY.

ADA: See AMERICANS WITH DISABILITIES ACT.

Additional Insured: An individual or organisation listed as covered by a primary insurance agreement.

Adjoining Rooms: Rooms with common walls, but without connecting doors.

Adult Learner: An adult who is usually pursuing education to attain a specific and practical goal.

Advance Order: An order for goods and/or services placed before the move-in date for an exhibition. Usually less expensive than an order made on-site or a FLOOR ORDER.

Advance Rate: Fees associated with advance orders, which typically include discounts when paid in advance.

Advance Registration: Booking before an event takes place. Allows attendees to register for an event before it actually takes place. See PRE-REGISTRATION.

Advisory Board: A group that offers advice or counsel to event organiser, event management, or other organisation on strategic options such as education content, exhibitor matters, contracting policies or other issues.

Affinity Group: Group sharing common interest, usually people who are members of the same organisation.

Agenda: A list or plan of items to be considered, decided, undertaken, or accomplished at a meeting or event. Agendas are generally formal, structured lists and may include a time schedule.

Agent: 1) Broadly, one who acts or has the power to act; more usually, one that acts as the representative of another. In travel, agent is specified by purpose, such as a retail travel agent. **2)** Person that obtains engagements for entertainers, is paid by the entertainers and has no contract for production responsibilities. **3)** Person in a speaker bureau/agency that acts on behalf of the seller (speaker) or on behalf of the buyer (customer).

Air Consignment Note: A BILL OF LADING that covers domestic and international flights transporting goods to a specified destination.

Air Wall: Movable, track-mounted barrier that partitions a large area such as a ballroom or exhibition hall into smaller sections. May be sound resistant, but not necessarily sound proof. Also known as a PARTITION.

Airfreight Forwarder: An airfreight company that transports freight via scheduled airlines. Forwarders do not operate their own planes.

Aisle: 1) Area between a booths/stands for attendee traffic movement. **2)** Space between tables or chairs to allow passage of an audience.

All-Risks Insurance: Insurance against loss of or damage to property arising from any fortuitous cause except those that are specifically excluded. .

Alternate Media: Alternatives to print materials (e.g. Braille, large print, etc.), telecommunications, computers, and other electronic media provided to assist people with disabilities in achieving full participation.

Alternative Dispute Resolution: Methods for resolving disputes without going to court.

Ambient Light: 1) Level of illumination from natural lighting sources already existing in an environment. **2)** Uncontrolled and unintended illumination.

Amenity: Complimentary items provided by a hotel in sleeping rooms such as toiletries, writing supplies, bathrobes, fruit baskets, and shoe shine mitts.

American Breakfast: A meal of fruits and/or juices, cereal, eggs, meat, bakery goods and hot or cold beverages.

American Hotel & Lodging Association (AH&LA): AH&LA is a member of the Convention Industry Council.

American Plan: A type of hotel rate that includes the price of the room and all meals. Also called FULL AMERICAN PLAN (FAP). See INCLUSIVE RATE.

American Service: Food is plated in the kitchen and placed before the guest. Side dishes are used for bread and butter and salad. Food is served from the left, beverages from the right, and all items are removed from the right. This is generally the service used for banquets. See PLATED SERVICE.

American Society of Association Executives (ASAE): ASAE & The Center of Association Leadership is a member of the Convention Industry Council.

American Society of Composers, Authors, and Publichers (ASCAP): A membership organisation that represents individuals who hold the copyrights to music written in the United States. ASCAP grants licensing agreements for the performance of that music.

Americans with Disabilities Act (ADA): U.S. legislation that prohibits discrimination against persons with disabilities in employment, transportation, public accommodations, communications and government activities.

Amphitheatre: An outdoor facility with a flat performance area surrounded by a sloped seating area for the audience. The seating area is usually a semi-circular shape or adapted to the surrounding landscape.

Amplifier: A device used to increase the sound levels of a signal to be sent to the loudspeakers for sound reproduction.

Analog: A method of conveying audio or video data electronically by varying its signal frequency or amplitude.

Andragogy: The art and science of helping adults learn as opposed to pedagogy, which is the science of helping children learn.

Application Service Provider (ASP): A company that provides software to customers through the Internet using centralized servers owned and managed by the provider.

Apron: Part of a stage in front of the main curtain.

Arbitration: Private dispute resolution process in which the parties agree to submit their dispute to an impartial third party for a decision. Depending on the type of arbitration, the arbitrator's decision may or may not be binding. A form of ALTERNATE DISPUTE RESOLUTION.

Arena: Facility type featuring a large flat main floor surrounded by fixed seats in a sloping oval or modified oval shape, much steeper that the typical theatre. Some are arranged in two or more tiers. Sight lines are nearly always designed for events the size of a hockey floor, circus, ice show, or basketball court.

Arrival/Departure Pattern: A description of arrival and departure activities of an event's attendees. This information should be included in the specifications guide for an event.

Aspect Ratio: The ratio of image width to height; pertaining to video and slides.

Assembly: 1) A general or formal meeting of an organisation attended by representatives of its members for the purpose of deciding legislative direction, policy matters, holding elections, or conducting governance business of the organisation. Consequently, an assembly usually observes certain rules of procedure for its meetings; generally prescribed in its Articles & By-laws. **2)** The process of erecting display component parts into a complete exhibit.

Association Management Company Institute (AMC Institute): AMCI is a member of the Convention Industry Council.

Association of Collegiate Conference and Events Directors - International (ACCED-I): ACCED-I is a member of the Convention Industry Council.

Association of Destination Management Executives International (ADMEI): ADMEI is a member of the Convention Industry Council.

Asymmetric Bandwidth: A term describing an Internet Service Provider (ISP) technology where the download and upload bandwidth are not equal.

Asynchronous Learning: Asynchronous learning is a student-centred teaching method that uses on-line learning resources to facilitate information sharing outside the constraints of time and place among a network of people. Typically this is on-demand and can be video-on-demand (VoD), audio-on-demand (AoD), correspondence courses, e-mail messages, bulletin boards, etc.

ATA Carnet: An international customs document that permits duty-free and tax-free temporary import of goods for up to one year. It eliminates or reduces value-added taxes (VAT) charges, customs fees, and bond fees. The acronym "ATA" represents the French and English words "Admission Temporaire/Temporary Admission." ATA carnets cover commercial samples, professional equipment, and goods for presentation or use at trade fairs, shows, exhibitions, etc. Items not covered are consumable or disposable goods that will not be returned home.

Attrition: The difference between the actual number of sleeping rooms (or food and beverage, or revenue) realized and the number agreed to in the facility's contract. Usually a percentage or actual shortfall limit is allowed before damages are assessed.

Audience Count: The total actual number of attendees at an event.

Audience Left and Right: Stage directions from the audience's perspective. This is the opposite of STAGE LEFT AND RIGHT. See also SCREEN LEFT AND RIGHT.

Audience Reaction Team: Four or five attendees query the main speaker from the stage with questions from the audience and follow-up questions.

Audience Response System: Interactive computer or mobile device application that enables voting or polling and then collects and displays the results.

Audioconference: A meeting using only voice transmissions between two or more sites.

Audiovisual (AV): AV includes equipment, materials, and teaching aids used in sound and visual presentations, such as video projection, monitors, sound equipment, etc. See EVENT TECHNOLOGY.

Audiovisual (AV) **Contractor:** Supplier of technical staff and audiovisual equipment (e.g. projectors, screens, sound systems, video, and staging).

Audiovisual (AV) **Technician:** An audiovisual professional who is responsible for the set-up, configuration or operation of lighting, sound, video, staging or other similar elements of an event function.

Audit: 1) A methodical examination and review of records pertaining to an event. For instance, an independent verification of attendance figures submitted by an exhibition's producers. **2)** An unbiased examination and evaluation of the financial statements of an organisation. It can be done internally (by employees of the organisation) or externally (by an outside firm).

Auditorium: Room for gathering an audience for speeches, performances, concerts etc. Often used to name entire facilities, though properly applied only to the seated portion of the facility in which the audience is assembled.

Auditorium Set-Up: Seating arrangement where chairs are arranged in rows facing head table, stage or speaker. Variations are semicircular and V-shaped. See THEATRE SET-UP.

Authorized Signatory: A person who is authorized to legally bind an individual or organisation to a contract, to sign cheques on behalf of an organisation, or charge to an organisation's master account.

Automated External Defibrilator (AED): Device installed in many large public areas (e.g. airports, hotels, convention centres). Can be used by any individual to administer life-saving care to person experiencing a heart attack.

Average Daily Room Rate (ADR): A measure of a hotel's financial performance that calculates the total sleeping room revenue for a given period's occupied rooms divided by the number of rooms occupied for the same period.

Average Room Rate: Mathematical average of a series of sleeping room rates.

Back Drape: A drape, curtain or fabric panel that provides a soft, colourful background for a speaker or stage presentation.

Back Light: 1) A light source that illuminates any transparent or translucent material from behind. **2)** A lighting instrument used behind and above a presenter to give more depth and better image to video projection or recording.

Back of House (BOH): A term used in hotels and other venues to refer to areas for staff only, as opposed to the front of the house.

Backbone: A permanently installed series of copper wire or fiber optic cabling that provides the main infrastructure for transmitting voice, data, and video signals within a facility.

Backdrop: Drapes, curtain, or fabric panels at the back of a stage, speaker's table, or exhibit booth/stand.

Backline Equipment: Equipment such as amplifiers and sound equipment required by musicians in order to perform at an engagement, often rented by the event organiser.

Backwall: 1) The back wall (either hardwall or draped) of a perimetre, booth/stand/exhibit, or inline. **2)** Panel arrangement at rear of booth/stand area.

Bandwidth: The amount of data that can be transmitted (upload) or received (download) per second. For additional bandwidth related terminology, see Appendix B: Bandwidth and Networking Terms for Meeting & Event Professionals.

Banquet: An elabourate, and often ceremonial, dinner for numerous people, often in honor of a particular person or persons.

Banquet Captain: Person in charge of banquet service at food functions. For small functions, may serve as maitre d. For larger functions, may be responsible for a specific area of the dining room.

Banquet Event Order (BEO): A form most often used by hotels to provide details to personnel concerned with a specific food and beverage function or event room set-up.

Banquet Manager: A person with overall responsibility for food and beverage delivery with direct staff (servers, banquet captains) and indirect (hotel kitchens and engineering).

Banquet Round: Round table used for meal service; depending on the diameter, can comfortably seat up to 12 persons. A round for 8 is usually 60-inches in diameter, and a round for 10 is usually 72-inches in diameter. Rounds that are 66 inches in diameter may also be found in use for tables of 8-10.

Banquet Set-Up: 1) Seating arrangement where typically a grouping of rounds is set in such a way as to facilitate the serving of food, most often a hexagonal or square pattern. **2)** Function-room set up and tear down. See HOUSEMAN.

BarCamp: These are participant-led conferences where everyone who attends contributes ademonstration or session, or otherwise volunteers in a way to contribute to the event.

Bare Booth/Stand: Booth/stand with no services or facilities, meaning that these all have to be hired at an additional cost.

Barn Door: Movable hinged flap used on stage lights to control light spill.

Base Currency: Currency in which all official business transactions will take place.

Base Plate: Plate used under bowl, glass, condiments, and so forth.

Batten: Lengths of pipe from which scenery, curtains, and lights can be hung.

Beaded Screen: Type of screen with highly reflective surface used for front projection.

Beamer: See LCD PROJECTOR.

Bed Tax: See TRANSIENT OCCUPANCY TAX.

Bell Captain: A hotel employee who supervises the work of staff whose primary responsibility is to carry luggage, run errands, etc.

Best Available Rate (BAR): Lowest available rate for non-group reservations at a hotel.

Bid: A proposal submitted by a convention & visitors bureau and/or hotel(s) or other suppliers to an event organiser that includes detailed specifications (such as dates, rates, concessions, etc.). Also known as a PROPOSAL.

Bill of Lading (B/L): A document that establishes the terms of a contract between a shipper and a transportation company under which freight is to be moved between specified points for a specified charge. It serves as a document of title, a contract of carriage, and a receipt of goods.

Billing Weight: Generally refers to airfreight and van line shipments. The billing weight is the number upon which freight charges are based. The billing weight will be the actual weight or the dimensional weight, whichever is greater.

Black Light: Ultraviolet lighting that when applied causes phosphorescent paints to glow.

Black Tie: Required dress: dinner jacket, bow tie and cummerbund for the men and formal evening dress for the women. May include national dress. In the U.S. and Canada, Black Tie indicates Tuxedo. "Black tie optional" indicates that formal dress is preferred but not required.

Blind Commission: A commission that is paid by a hotel to a third party for services; it comes out of the hotel sleeping room rate, but is not disclosed to the guests or the event organiser. In some countries, this practice could be subject to legal restrictions and/or ethical concerns.

Blue Laws: Laws that regulate the types of businesses that must be closed, or the types of products that may not be sold, on Sundays. Also known as Sunday Laws.

Blueline: Final review copy for client's approval before printing. Also referred to as a proof.

Boardroom: A room set permanently in a conference configuration, generally with a fixed table and executive seating.

Boardroom Set-Up: Seating arrangement in which rectangle or oval shaped tables are set up with chairs on both sides and ends. Often confused with HOLLOW SQUARE SET-UP.

Bonded Warehouse: A warehouse authorized by customs authorities for storage of goods on which payment of duties is deferred until the goods are removed.

Bonding: The purchase, for a premium, of a guarantee of protection for a supplier or a customer. In the hospitality industry, certain bonding programmes are mandatory.

Boneyard: Storage area where equipment is stored during an exhibition. This area may be located within the exhibition hall in an unused portion of the floor.

Booking Policy: Guidelines by which a convention centre (or other venue) prioritizes reservations; may correspond to hotel rooms the event will use in the area.

Booth: Specific exhibit display area assigned by show management to an exhibitor under contractual agreement. Internationally, the term STAND is used. See STAND.

Brainstorming: Group sessions in which all participants contribute creative ideas which are not initially judged for merit.

Break: Short interval between sessions at which time coffee, tea and/or other refreshments are served. See also REFRESHMENT BREAK.

Break-Even Point: The point at which revenues are equal to expenses.

Break-Out Rooms: Function rooms set up for a group within an event as opposed to a plenary or general session spaces. Also known as SYNDICATE ROOMS.

Break-Out Sessions: Small group sessions, panels, workshops or presentations, offered concurrently within an event. Break-Out Sessions occur apart from the general session.

Broadcast Music, Incorporated (BMI): A music licensing organisation that represents individuals who hold the copyrights to music written in the United States. It grants licensing agreements for the performance of music.

Broadcast Producer: Person who oversees the production and broadcast of a virtual or hybrid event.

Broker: A non-asset based transportation provider that sells transportation services for commercial shippers. Brokers commonly use freight forwarders.

Budget: A statement of estimated revenues and expenditures for a specified period of time, event or project; divided into subject categories and arranged by principal areas of revenue and expense.

Budget Philosophy: Financial goal of the event (break-even, profit or expense).

Buffet: Assortment of foods, offered on a table, self-served.

Butler Service: 1) Servers offer a variety of both hot and cold hors d'oeuvres on platters to guests at receptions. **2)** A style of table service where guests serve themselves from platters presented by the server. 3) Specialized in-room service offered by a hotel, resort or cruise ship.

Buying Agent: An agent who purchases goods on behalf of a company or agency.

Buzz Session: Method to increase audience participation by dividing all participants in discussion groups each of which reports the group's findings and opinions during a following plenary session.

By the Bottle: Liquor served and charged for by the full bottle.

By the Drink: See ON CONSUMPTION.

By the Person: Per Person. A fixed price per attendee; covers all consumption of food and beverage at a function, within a given time frame.

By the Piece: Food purchased by the individual piece, usually for a reception.

Cabana: Room adjacent to pool area, with or without sleeping facilities.

Cabaret Set-up: 1) Room arrangement with cocktail tables, chairs and a stage. **2)** Outside of North America, refers to seating at round tables with chairs placed at two thirds to three quarters of the table and no seating with backs to the speaker. See also CRESCENT-ROUND SET-UP and HALF MOON SET-UP.

Cabaret Table: Small round table, 15- 30 inches in diameter (38-76 centimetres) used for cocktail type parties. Also called COCKTAIL TABLE.

Cafeteria Service: A food service operation in which customers carry their own trays and select food from a display counter or counters. Payment is sometimes made at a cashier station.

Call Brand: Brand of liquor, distinguished from HOUSE BRAND, selected by a customer according to personal preference. Usually a higher quality than house brands.

Call for Papers: An invitation to submit topic ideas for the conference programme. Document containing detailed instructions for submission of papers for assessment and selection by a review committee; often referred to as "Abstract Forms." Also known as "Call for Presentations". See ABSTRACT. See also CONFERENCE PAPERS.

Campus Housing: Dormitory or other university/college sleeping accommodations.

Cancellation Clause: Provision in a contract which outlines damages to be paid to the non-cancelling party if cancellation occurs, due the cancelling party's breach of the contract.

Cancellation or Interruption Insurance: Insurance that protects a event organiser against financial loss or expenses incurred when contractually specified perils necessitate cancelling or relocating a event, or cause a reduction in attendance.

Cancellation/No-Show Percentage: The number or percentage of contracted rooms that do not actualize into occupied rooms due to guest cancellations or no-shows. See also ATTRITION, WASH.

Cancelled Business: Business that was confirmed definite by contract and was later cancelled.

Captain: See BANQUET CAPTAIN.

Carbon Neutral : Carbon neutral is the point at which enough carbon is offset or sequestered to cover a specific amount of carbon generated by a manufacturing process, transportation method, product usage, building or individual.

Cargo Insurance: Additional coverage protecting the owner of goods for loss or damage while goods are in a carrier's possession. Recommended for all international shipments.

Carnet: A customs document permitting the holder to carry or send merchandise temporarily into certain foreign countries (for display, demonstration or similar purposes) without paying duties or posting bonds.

Cartage: 1) Fee charged for transporting freight between destinations. **2)** Short distance hauling of exhibit properties.

Cash Accounting: An accounting method that records income and expenses at the time when payment is received or expenses are paid. Compare with ACCRUAL ACCOUNTING.

Cash Bar: Private room bar set up where guests pay for drinks individually.

Cash Basis Accounting: See CASH ACCOUNTING. Compare with ACCRUAL ACCOUNTING.

Casualty Insurance: A type of insurance that is primarily concerned with the legal liability for losses caused by injury to persons or damage to the property of others.

Category Cable: (Unshielded Twisted Pair Cable or UTP) Usually referred to as Cat followed by a numeral between and 1 and 7. Cat 5 or Cat 5e cabling, required for Fast Ethernet, is the most commonly available. See BACKBONE.

Catering Sales Manager: Staff person responsible for selling and servicing group and local food and beverage functions.

Ceiling Height: Maximum height of ceiling of an exhibition hall or event room.

Centre for Exhibition Industry Research (CEIR): CEIR is a member of the Convention Industry Council.

Centre Speakers: Loudspeakers that are used to cover assignments out of the range of the main loudspeakers' projection area.

Certificate in Meeting Management (CMM): Certificate offered by the Global Business Travel Association and Meeting Professionals International.

Certificate of Insurance: A document provided by an insurance company as proof that a policy has been issued and coverage is in effect.

Certificate of Origin: A document, required by certain countries for tariff purposes, certifying as to the country of origin of specified goods.

Certified Association Executive (CAE): Certification offered by the American Society of Association Executives and ASAE University. Another CAE certification is offered by the Canadian Society of Association Executives.

Certified Destination Marketing Executive (CDME): Certification offered by Destination Marketing Association International (DMAI).

Certified Exhibition Manager (CEM): Certification offered by the International Association of Exhibitions and Events (IAEE).

Certified Hospitality Marketing Executive (CHME): Certification offered by the Hospitality Sales & Marketing Association International (HSMAI).

Certified Hospitality Sales Professional (CHSP): Certification offered by the American Hotel & Lodging Educational Institute.

Certified Hotel Administrator (CHA): Certification offered by the American Hotel & Lodging Educational Institute.

Certified Incentive Travel Executive (CITE): A designation offered by the Society for Incentive Travel Excellence (SITE).

Certified Manager of Exhibits (CME): Certification offered by the Trade Show Exhibitors Association (TSEA).

Certified Meeting Professional (CMP): Certification offered by the Convention Industry Council (CIC).

Certified Professional Catering and Events (CPCE): Certification offered by the National Association of Catering Executives (NACE).

Certified Speaking Professional (CSP): Certification offered by the National Speakers Association (NSA).

Certified Special Events Professional (CSEP): Certification offered by the International Special Event Society (ISES).

Certified Weight: An official weight issued from a Certified Weight Master. This individual certifies a shipment's weight as the only acceptable weight for transportation and material handling at a tradeshow.

Change Order: Facility form to advise departments of changes in reservations or functions.

Chart of Accounts: A detailed list of the individual line items that make up the revenue and expense categories in a budget. A numbering system used to identify every line item in a budget, so income and expenses are posted to the correct accounts.

Charter: 1) Exclusive use of all or some space on an airplane, bus, ship, or other vehicle for a special period of time and for a specific itinerary. **2)** To create a new association, organisation or chapter of an association or organisation.

Check-In Time: Time at which hotel guests may check in and occupy sleeping rooms.

Check-Out Time: Time by which hotel guests are required to vacate sleeping rooms.

Cherry Picker: Equipment capable of lifting a person or persons to a given height.

Chevron Set-Up: Seating arrangement in which chairs /or chairs or tables are arranged in rows slanted in a V shape and separated by a centre aisle. They face the head table or speaker. See HERRINGBONE SET-UP. See also V-SHAPE SET-UP.

Citywide Event: An event that requires the use of a convention centre or event complex, as well as multiple hotels in the host city.

Classroom Set-Up: Seating arrangement in which rows of tables with chairs face the front of a room and each person has a space for writing. Also called SCHOOLROOM SET-UP.

Classroom Table: Rectangular table, often narrower than regular tables and 30-inches high. Can be 6' or 8' long and 18- or 24-inches wide.

Clean Bill of Lading: A receipt for goods issued by a carrier with an indication that the goods were received in apparent good order and condition, without damages or other irregularities. See FOUL BILL OF LADING.

Clean Draft: A draft to which no documents have been attached.

Clear Date/Time: Generally the last point in time at which an exhibitor-appointed carrier must be in line or at the dock in order to be loaded after the close of the show.

Clinic: Workshop-type educational experience where participants learn by doing.

Closed-Ended Incentive Programmes: The number of winners are limited by a predetermined amount to be spent on the incentive programme. See also OPEN-ENDED INCENTIVE Programmes.

Closing Ceremony: Final activities at an event which occur during the closing or last session.

Closing Session: The final session of an event in which the subjects which have been discussed are summarized and possible conclusions reached and announced.

Co-Location: To hold two or more related events at the same time and in the same place.

Cocktail Table: Small round table, 15- 30 inches in diameter (38-76 centimetres) and 30 inches in height (76 centimetres) used for cocktail parties. Also called CABARET TABLE.

Collateral: 1) The promotional material used by the salespeople to support or corroborate the features and benefits of the item being sold. **2)** Collective term for material distributed to attendees at registration, including badges, lanyards, tote bags, agenda and other materials. **3)** Assets that can be pledged to guarantee a loan.

Collection and Consolidation Service: Service performed for a shipper in which a number of smaller shipments are picked up or received and forwarded as one truckload shipment.

Colloquium: An informal meeting for the purpose of discussion; usually of an academic or research nature and in order to ascertain areas of mutual interest through exchange of ideas. Conducted as and when convenient, but with little regularity.

Commission: A payment made to an individual or organisation for bringing business to another individual or organisation.

Commissionable Rate Commitment: A contract in which the room rate to be charged to attendees includes a commission to be paid to either the sponsoring group or a third party such as a travel agent or independent event planning or site selection organisation.

Committee: A group of people appointed for a specific function, typically consisting of members of a larger group.

Common Carrier: Transportation company which handles materials; an agency or business that is available to the public for transportation of persons or goods; usually referring to freight transportation on regularly scheduled trucks or airplanes.

Complete Meeting Package (CMP): An all-inclusive plan offered by conference centres; includes lodging, all meals and support services.

Complimentary Ratio: The number of rooms provided at no cost based on the number of occupied rooms. Often expressed numerically, for example 1/50, 1:50 or 1- per-50.

Compression/Decompression or Coder/Decoder (CODEC): Videoconferencing standard, included in hardware and/or software, used to compress or code video, audio, and data signals for transmission and decompress or decode the signal at the other end of the transmission.

Computer Aided Design and Manufacturing (CAD/CAM): Software used to design and manufacture products.

Concessions: 1) Merchandise or refreshments sold on site, to individuals, in conjunction with an event. **2)** Contractual agreement where one party provides something of value to the other party in exchange for something else, pending certain conditions.

Conclave: Gathering of a group with shared or special interests. Traditionally refers to meetings of a confidential or secret nature with restricted or limited participation. From the Latin for "with key", referring to a historical practice of sequestering participants.

Concurrent Sessions: Multiple sessions scheduled at the same time. Programmes on different themes or subjects offered simultaneously.

Conference: 1) Participatory meeting designed for discussion, fact-finding, problem solving and consultation. **2)** An event used by any organisation to meet and exchange views, convey a message, open a debate or give publicity to some area of opinion on a specific issue. No tradition, continuity or timing is required to convene a conference. Conferences are usually of short duration with specific objectives, and are generally on a smaller scale than congresses or conventions. See CONGRESS. See also CONVENTION.

Conference Centre: A facility that provides a dedicated environment for events, especially small events. May be certified by the International Association of Conference Centres.

Conference Officer/Organiser: Title generally conferred upon the chief administrator of the entire event. See also PROFESSIONAL CONGRESS ORGANISER (PCO).

Conference Services Manager (CSM): Primary contact person assigned to an event in a hotel or convention centre. Also referred to as CONVENTION SERVICES MANAGER.

Conference Set-Up: Seating arrangement in which rectangular or oval tables are set up with chairs placed around all sides.

Confirmed Letter of Credit: A letter of credit, issued by a foreign bank, whose validity has been confirmed by a second bank. An exporter whose payment terms are a confirmed letter of credit is assured of payment even if the foreign buyer or the foreign bank defaults. See LETTER OF CREDIT.

Congress: 1) The regular coming together of large groups of individuals, generally to discuss a particular subject. A congress will often last several days and have several simultaneous sessions. The length of time between congresses is usually annual, although some are on a less frequent basis. Most international or world congresses are latter type; national congresses are more frequently held annually. **2)** European term for convention. See CONFERENCE and CONVENTION.

Congress Centre: A facility, typically outside the U.S, that hosts trade shows and other large functions which contains a large exhibition hall and additional small meeting and event spaces.

Connecting Rooms: In a hotel, a configuration of two or more guest rooms with private connecting doors permitting access between rooms without exiting into a public corridor.

Consecutive Interpretation: Oral translation of several phrases or entire speeches from one language to another. Speaker pauses between phrases to allow for interpretation. See INTERPRETATION IN RELAY, SIMULTANEOUS INTERPRETATION, WHISPERED INTERPRETATION, WIRELESS INFRARED INTERPRETING SYSTEM.

Consideration: The inducement to a contract. The cause, motive, price, or impelling influence which induces a contracting party to enter a contract.

Consignee: Recipient. The person, people, or organisation to whom something is delivered or addressed. Compare with CONSIGNOR.

Consignor: A person who sends freight. Compare with CONSIGNEE.

Consular Declaration: A formal statement describing goods to be shipped; filed with and approved by the consul of the country of destination prior to shipment.

Consular Invoice: A document, required by some countries, describing a shipment of goods and showing information such as the consignor, consignee, and value of the shipment. Certified by a consular official of the foreign country, it is used by that country's customs officials to verify the value, quantity, and nature of the shipment.

Consumer Show: Exhibition that is open to the public, usually requiring an entrance fee. See EXHIBITION, GATE SHOW, PUBLIC SHOW. Compare with TRADE SHOW.

Container Detention: A charge that is assessed when a container is not returned to the carrier within the allowable time.

Continental Breakfast: Light morning meal consisting of pastries, juices, and hot beverages. May also include fruit. Usually served buffet style.

Continental Plan: A room rate that includes a continental breakfast. See also AMERICAN PLAN, DEMI-PENSION, EUROPEAN PLAN, MODIFIED AMERICAN PLAN.

Continuing Education: Structured educational and training experiences for personal or professional development.

Continuing Education Credit (CEC): Requirement of many professional groups by which members must certify participation in formal educational programmes designed to maintain their level of ability beyond their original certification date. See CONTINUING EDUCATION UNIT (CEU).

Continuing Education Unit (CEU): Non-academic credit unit conferred by professional organisations for formal educational programmes for members who must maintain their level of professional education.

Contract: An agreement between two or more parties that creates in each party a duty to do or not do something and a right to performance of the other's duty or a remedy for the breach of the other's duty. See also LETTER OF AGREEMENT.

Contract Carrier: Trucking company that enters into a specific contract with a shipper to transport goods for an agreed-upon price. Contained within the contract are all the terms and conditions, liability, transit times, etc.

Controversy Panel: To stimulate interest and debate, arrange for two or three views of a controversial issue to be presented.

Convenor: Member of committee in charge of convening participants.

Convention: Gathering of delegates, representatives, and members of a membership or industry organisation convened for a common purpose. Common features include educational sessions, committee meetings, social functions, and meetings to conduct the governance business of the organisation. Conventions are typically recurring events with specific, established timing.

Convention & Visitors Authority (CVA): See CONVENTION AND VISITORS BUREAU.

Convention and Visitors Bureau (CVB): An organisation defined and recognized by it's status as an incorporated, non-profit agency or local government entity which promotes economic development of the community through travel and tourism. CVBs assist planners by providing information on local resources and services, site selection, and other pre-conference and post-convention services. See also DESTINATION MARKETING ORGANISATION.

Convention Centre: Facility whose purpose it is to host trade shows, public shows, conventions, and other functions and that combines exhibition space with a substantial number of smaller meeting and event spaces. A convention centre may be purpose-built or converted and municipally or privately owned.

Convention Industry Council (CIC): A federation of national and international organisations representing individuals, firms or properties involved in the meetings, conventions, exhibitions, and travel and tourism industries.

Convention Sales Professionals International (CSPI): CSPI is a member of the Convention Industry Council.

Convention Services Manager (CSM): Professional at a hotel, convention centre or convention bureau who is responsible for event operations management on all levels.

Copyright: Laws that allow for the ownership of intellectual property (such as writings, art, music). Copy-written material may not be used without the owner's permission or the payment of royalty fees.

Corkage: A charge placed on beer, liquor, and wine brought into a facility but purchased elsewhere.

Corner Booth/Stand: An exhibit space with exposure on at least two aisles, often sold by show managers at a premium rate.

Corporate Event Marketing Association (CEMA): CEMA is a member of the Convention Industry Council.

Corporate Rate: Special rate for sleeping rooms or other goods and services that is made available to business travellers. These rates may vary by corporation, depending on the negotiated agreement.

Corporate Travel: The market segment comprised of groups or individuals that work for a given company and are travelling for business reasons at the company's expense.

Cost and Freight (C&F): A pricing term indicating that these costs are included in the quoted price.

Cost and Insurance (C&I): A pricing term indicating that these costs are included in the quoted price.

Cost, Insurance, Freight (CIF): A pricing term indicating that these costs are included in the quoted price.

Cost, Insurance, Freight and Commission (CIF&C): A pricing term indicating that these costs are included in the quoted price.

Cost, Insurance, Freight and Exchange (CIF&E): A pricing term indicating that these costs are included in the quoted price.

Countervailing Duty: An import duty imposed to offset export grants, bounties, or subsidies paid to foreign suppliers in certain countries by the governments of those countries as an incentive to exports.

Country of Origin: A person's country of natural birth or citizenship; an item's country of manufacture, production, or agricultural growth.

Courier: 1) European term for a travel professional who supervises arrival details and escorts tours. **2)** A person or service who delivers messages, packages or mail.

Cover: 1) Table setting for one person. **2)** Actual number of meals, or servings, served at a food function. **3)** Dome placed over a plate, used to keep food warm/cold.

Covers: Actual number of meals served at a catered meal function or in a restaurant.

Credentials Committee: Committee formed to verify that individuals have the necessary qualifications to attend a meeting, cast votes at a meeting, or become a member of an association.

Crescent-Round Set-Up: Seating at round tables with chairs placed at two thirds to three quarters of the table and no seating with backs to the speaker. Used for banquet-to-meeting or meeting-to-banquet quick set. See also CABARET SET-UP and HALF MOON SET-UP.

Cross Aisle: An smaller aisle perpendicular to a larger main aisle.

Customs: The governmental authorities designated to collect duties levied by a country on imports and exports. The term also applies to the procedures involved in such collection.

Customs Broker: An individual or company, that is licensed by the government to enter and clear goods through customs.

Customs House: An individual or firm licensed to enter and clear goods through customs.

Cut-Off Date: Designated date when a hotel will release any unsold sleeping rooms in a group block and make them available to the general public. See RESERVATION REVIEW DATE.

Cut-Off Time: A specific point in time at which the exhibition contractor will cease (for the day) all unloading or loading activities. In transportation environment this refers to the specific time a shipment must be tendered to a carrier in order to receive service that day. For example, a flight that departs at 10:00 p.m. may have a cargo cut-off time of 7:00 p.m.

Dais: Raised platform usually above the floor of a hall or large room. See PODIUM. See also RISER.

Damage Clause: Part of a contract dealing with procedures, penalties, and rights of the party causing damages.

Data Projector: See LCD PROJECTOR.

Debate: A discussion which takes place within a meeting, a public or private sitting or in one of the various types of assembly or meeting.

Declared Value: Shipper's stated value of entire shipment in terms of dollars.

Décor: Props, lighting, or other decorative elements used to create a theme, ambiance or mood at a function or special event.

Decorator: An individual or company providing installation & dismantle and booth/stand and hall dressing services for a trade show and/or its exhibitors. Decorator services may be provided by carpenters, sign painters or others depending upon union jurisdiction. Term applies to both contractor and skilled craftsperson.

Dedicated Bandwidth: A set amount of BANDWIDTH that is exclusively available to the end user or group.

Definite Booking: Space reservations confirmed in writing.

Delay Speakers: Loudspeakers that are used to cover assignments out of the range of the main loudspeakers' projection area.

Delegate: Outside of North America, a general term for registered meeting participant. In some instances a voting representative at a meeting.

Demi-Pension: A rate inclusive of breakfast and dinner, in addition to the room. In the U.S. and Canada it is called MODIFIED AMERICAN PLAN (MAP), which means breakfast and one other meal (usually dinner). See also AMERICAN PLAN, CONTINENTAL PLAN, EUROPEAN PLAN.

Destination Management Company (DMC): A professional services company possessing extensive local knowledge, expertise and resources, specializing in the design and implementation of events, activities, tours, transportation and programme logistics.

Destination Management Certified Professional (DMCP): Certification offered by the Association of Destination Management Executives (ADME).

Destination Marketing Association International (DMAI): DMAI is a member of the Convention Industry Council.

Destination Marketing Organisation (DMO): An organisation defined and recognized by it's status as an incorporated, non-profit agency or local government entity which promotes economic development of the community through travel and tourism. CVBs assist planners by providing information on local resources and services, site selection, and other pre-conference and post-convention services. See also CONVENTION AND VISITORS BUREAU.

Dine Around: Use of a number of restaurants in a destination with reservations and billing arrangements to one particular client.

Direct Spending: All expenditures associated with an event that flow into the host destination's local economy. Direct spending includes attendee spending, exhibitor spending and event organiser spending. See also ECONOMIC IMPACT, INDIRECT SPENDING, & INDUCED SPENDING.

Discussion Group: A group of participants assigned to debate or explore a topic within some types of meetings. Similar to a working group, but typically without an expectation for formal reports or papers.

Display Rules & Regulations: A set of specifications for exhibit construction endorsed by all major exhibit industry associations. Also refers to the individual additional rules which may be adopted by event management. Guidelines are provided by the International Association of Exhibition Executives.

Distance Learning: Virtual Learning: Education delivered through a variety of technological and communication methods, including, but not limited to: e-mail, e-learning platforms, web conferencing, mobile apps and podcasts.

DMC Consortium: National and/or international alliances of destination management companies that form select communities for the purpose of sharing collective efforts for business sharing, education, ethics and destination management industry monitoring.

Dock Receipt: A receipt issued by an ocean carrier to acknowledge receipt of a shipment at the carrier's dock or warehouse facilities.

Double Booking: 1) Reserving space for two groups to use the same space at the same time and neither can be fully accommodated as contracted. **2)** An organisation reserving space in more than one venue for the same event. **3)** Two or more reservations made for the same traveller for the same dates.

Double Cloth: Use of two tablecloths on a banquet table for decorative purposes, to muffle sound, or to attach to skirting. Usually two different colours are used. See OVERLAY.

Double Occupancy: A hotel guest room that may be occupied by two persons.

Double Room Rate: The price per person for a double-occupancy hotel guest room.

Double-Double Room: A hotel guest room with two double beds.

Downstage: Front of the stage, closest to the audience.

Dram Shop Laws: In the United States, a term for laws covering the liability of people serving alcoholic beverages. Under dram shop laws, a party injured by an intoxicated person can sue establishments contributing to that person's intoxication.

Draped Booth/Stand: A booth/stand where the back and side walls are constructed using pipe and drape (typically provided by management).

Drayage: See MATERIAL HANDLING.

Dress Code: A set of standards to provide guidance about what is appropriate to wear for an occasion, event or place of employment.

Dressing the Exhibit: Placing graphics, plants, literature and applying any finishing touches to the display.

Duty: Fee levied on imported and exported goods. Duties are generally based on the value of the goods (ad valorem duties), some other factors such as weight or quantity (specific duties), or a combination of value and other factors (compound duties). See AD VALOREM TAX.

E-Poster System: A system that uses a large monitor and computer to display multimedia versions of a poster; typically used at scientific and medical conferences.

Early Arrival: 1) To reach your destination before the appointed date or time. **2)** When a hotel guest with a confirmed reservation requests to check in to his/her room prior to the scheduled date and/or check-in time. **3)** Arrival prior to arrival of the majority of the group.

Early Registration: Registration received before a pre-defined date, usually offering a lower fee.

Early-Out: A guest who checks out of a hotel one or more days earlier than the scheduled departure date. Also called early departure, under-stay, UNEXPECTED DEPARTURE. Compare with OVERSTAY.

Economic Impact (Total): The total value of an event, including secondary spending (indirect and induced) on the host destination's local economy over and above the original direct spending. These secondary impacts, when combined with the original direct spending, result in the total economic impact of an event. See also DIRECT SPENDING, INDIRECT SPENDING AND INDUCED SPENDING.

Economic Multiplier: Total economic impact divided by direct spending. See also ECONOMIC IMPACT, DIRECT SPENDING.

Electronic Request for Proposal (E-RFP): Requests for proposals that are generated using on-line tools, including those from meeting technology suppliers and hotel websites; often used for site selection as well as other sourcing for event products and services.

Ellipsoidal Spotlight: A spotlight that can be shaped and controlled to light lecterns, signs and areas that need a tightly focused light pool; can be used with a gobo to project images such as a logo. See also LEKO.

Emergency Action Plan: Procedures about how to react and respond to an emergency situation, such as medical emergencies, fire and bomb threats.

Empty Sticker: The tag indicating a crate may be moved into storage. The sticker identifies the exhibitor and the return location for the crate.

End Cap: An exhibit space with aisles on three sides. See PENINSULA.

English Breakfast: A large, hearty breakfast that includes juice, fruit, hot and cold cereal, eggs, meat (often fish), pastries with jellies and preserves, and made to order foods such as omelettes and crêpes, and hot beverages.

English Service: Food is brought to the table on a tray, presented to the host, who either cuts the food him/herself or chooses to have it done by the server away from the table. Vegetables are placed in bowls on the table for guests to serve themselves. See FAMILY-STYLE SERVICE.

Entertainment: Activity performed for the amusement and enjoyment of others.

Errors and Omissions (E&O) **Insurance:** A form of insurance that indemnifies the insured for any loss sustained because of an error or oversight on his part.

Escorted Tour: 1) A prearranged travel programme, usually for a group. In a fully conducted tour, escort and/or guide service is provided throughout. **2)** A sightseeing programme conducted by a guide (e.g. a city tour). See TOUR. See also ESCORT.

European Plan (EP) **:** A room rate that does not include meals. Compare with AMERICAN PLAN, INCLUSIVE RATE.

Evaluation: 1) Critiquing and rating the overall success of an event. **2)** A systematic process to determine the value of an activity.

Event: An organised occasion such as a meeting, convention, exhibition, special event, gala dinner, etc. An event is often composed of several different yet related FUNCTIONS.

Event Organiser: Person whose job it is to oversee and arrange every aspect of an event. Person can be an employee or hired ad hoc to plan, organise, implement, and control meetings, conventions, and other events. See also PCO, PROFESSIONAL CONGRESS ORGANISER.

Event Service Professionals Association (ESPA): ESPA is a member of the Convention Industry Council.

Event Site: Premises where an event will be held. See SITE.

Event Specifications Guide (ESG): The preferred term for a comprehensive document that outlines the complete requirements and instructions for an event. This document is typically authored by the event planner and is shared with all appropriate vendors as a vehicle to communicate the expectations of services for a project. Sometimes called staging guide, RÉSUMÉ.

Event Technology: Any technical and technology needs to support meeting or events. Includes items such as audio-visual, computers, software, power, networking and connectivity

Event-Contracted Block (ECB): The rooms that are contracted by an event organiser with a hotel(s) or housing facility(s) for a particular event.

Exclusive: Any agreement which limits who may provide specific products or services under certain conditions to only one party. No other contractor is allowed to provide the same services or products in that facility.

Exclusive Contract: Contract between a facility and a service provider designating that provider as the only source of a specific service or product within that facility.

Exclusive Contractor: Contractor appointed by event or building management as the sole agent to provide specific services or products.

Executive Conference Centre (ECC): A first class conference facility that caters to executive level events.

Exhibit Booth/Stand: Individual display area constructed to showcase products or convey a message, or to sell products or services.

Exhibit Hall: Area within a facility where an exhibition is located; usually designed specifically for large shows.

Exhibit House: Company that fabricates and manages display properties for trade show exhibitors.

Exhibit Manager: See EXHIBITION MANAGER.

Exhibition: An event at which products, services or promotional materials are displayed to attendees visiting exhibits on the show floor. These events focus primarily on business-to-business (B2B) relationships. Also known as EXHIBITION, FAIR, TRADE FAIR, TRADE SHOW. Compare with: CONSUMER SHOW, GATE SHOW, PUBLIC SHOW.

Exhibition Manager: Preferred term for the specific person responsible for all aspects of planning, promoting, and producing an exhibition. Also called EXHIBIT MANAGER, SHOW MANAGER, SHOW ORGANISER.

Exhibition Services & Contractors Association (ESCA): ESCA is a member of the Convention Industry Council. (Formerly known as ACOM.)

Exhibitor: 1) Person or firm that displays its products or services at an event. **2)** Event attendee whose primary purpose for attending the event is to staff a booth/stand.

Exhibitor Advisory Committee: Representatives of an event's exhibiting companies who act as advisors to show management on procedures, the needs of exhibitors, and provide feedback for marketing and growing the show.

Exhibitor Appointed Contractor (EAC): Any company other than the designated "official" contractor providing a service to an exhibitor. Can refer to an Install & Dismantle Company (I&D House), photographer, florist or any other type of contractor.

Exhibitor Kit: See EXHIBITOR MANUAL.

Exhibitor Move-In/Move-out: The time period allowed for exhibitors to prepare their exhibit space for show opening. The time allowed for exhibitors to dismantle and remove their exhibit following show closing.

Exhibitor Prospectus: Promotional materials sent to current and prospective exhibitors to encourage participation. It promotes the value of exhibiting in a specific show and contains information about technical points, cost of exhibition space, a floor plan of the exhibition and an application for participation.

Exhibitor Service Kit: See EXHIBITOR MANUAL.

Exhibitor Service Manual: Manual or kit, usually developed by the GENERAL SERVICE CONTRACTOR for an event, containing general event information, labour/service order forms, rules and regulations and other information pertinent to an exhibitor's participation in an exhibition. Also called EXHIBITOR SERVICE KIT or EXHIBITOR KIT.

Export Declaration: A government customs document used to declare designated good to be shipped out of a country. Used for export control and compilation of foreign trade data.

Export License: A government document which permits the "licensee" to engage in the export of designated goods to certain destinations.

Exposition: A large public show, exhibit, or trade show; also referred to as an EXHIBITION.

Facilitator: An individual who guides discussion and/or decision making.

Facility: A structure that is built, installed or established to serve a particular purpose.

Facility Manager: The manager of a convention centre, exhibition hall, arena, auditorium or other venue or assembly.

Fair: 1) Event principally devoted to the exhibition of agricultural products or industrial products. Fairs may also provide entertainment activities. 2) Exhibition of products or services in a specific area of activity held with the objective of promoting business.

Familiarization (FAM) **Trip:** A programme designed to acquaint potential buyers with specific destinations or services and to stimulate the booking of an event. Often offered in groups, but sometimes on an individual basis. Also known as Fam trip or Fam.

Family-Style Service: Platters and bowls of foods are set on the dining tables, from which guests serve themselves. Usually involves guests passing the containers to each other. See ENGLISH SERVICE.

Fast Fold Screen: Brand name for a large screen with a frame which folds down into a small case for storage. The legs of this screen are attached at the sides of the screen, or the screen may be flown from above.

Federacion de Entidades Organizadores De Congresos Y Afines de America Latina (COCAL): COCAL is a member of the Convention Industry Council.

Fill-Type Speakers: Loudspeakers that are used to cover assignments out of the range of the main loudspeakers' projection area.

Final Programme: Document containing the definitive conference and social programme, circulated immediately prior to an event or distributed at the commencement of the event.

Financial and Insurance Conference Planners (FICP): FICP is a member of the Convention Industry Council.

Fire Exit: Door or passageway, clear of obstructions, designed by local authorities for egress from a building or structure.

Fire Marshal: 1) In the United States and Canada, the fire marshal is typically a member of the fire department whose duties include fire code enforcement. 2) In the United Kingdom, fire marshals are civilians trained to assist with fire evacuation procedures.

First Option: See OPTION.

Fishbowl: An interchange between an inner circle debating an issue and an outer circle of observers. Individuals occasionally move from one circle to the other.

Fishpole: Holder with microphone often used in Q & A (question and answer) sessions.

Fixed Assets: Usually non-liquid assets that are integral to the enterprise's day-to-day business operations (e.g. factories, equipment, furniture and real estate).

Fixed Costs: The day-to-day cost of doing business that is pre-committed, such as salaries, insurance, lease expenses, utilities, etc.

Fixed Expense: Expense incurred regardless of the number of event attendees.

Flash Box: Smoke-producing device for special effects.

Flat Rate: Rate for which a hotel agrees to offer any of its available sleeping rooms (with the exception of suites) to a group. Final assignment of rooms is at the discretion of the hotel. See RUN-OF-HOUSE.

Floor Load: Maximum amount of weight per square foot/metre a floor can support.

Floor Manager: Person retained by event management to supervise the installation, dismantling and operation of the exhibit area.

Floor Marking: The process of marking the floor of an empty exhibit hall to indicate the locations where individual booths/stands will be set.

Floor Order: Order for exhibitor services placed on-site after exhibit set up begins. Usually more expensive than an ADVANCE ORDER.

Floor Plan: 1) Scale drawing indicating the placement of exhibit booths and all other features in an exhibit hall. 2) Scale drawing of the floor area of a hotel's event space. 3) Scale drawing of a function room with specific set-up requirements (tables, chairs, etc.) drawn to scale.

Fly: Objects, scenery or audio-visual equipment mounted from above.

Focus Group: Qualitative method of research utilizing a small selection of representatives from a larger stakeholder group. Led by a facilitator, focus group members share their thoughts on an issue or product.

Follow Spot: Movable spotlight (a brilliant light projected onto a particular area).

Force Majeure: An event (e.g. war, labour strike, extreme weather, or other disruptive circumstances) or effect that cannot be reasonably anticipated or avoided.

Force Majeure Clause: A clause in an agreement that excuses performance in the event that a FORCE MAJEURE makes the performance impracticable or impossible.

Forced Freight: Forced freight is generally removed from the hall at a specified time and held by the general contractor or official common carrier or until payment is made for forwarding.

Forcing the Floor: Removal of freight from the event floor, after the event close, that was not picked up by an exhibitor's carrier, or shipments left behind at the booth/stand at the close of the event without a bill of lading.

Foreign Exchange Currency Risk: Risk that an organisation takes when dealing with foreign currency due to exchange rates fluctuating over time.

Foreign Sales Agent: An individual or firm that serves as an international representative of, and seeks sales abroad for, a domestic company.

Foreign Trade Zone: A geographic area where goods may be landed, handled, and reexported without being subject to import duty. See also BONDED WAREHOUSE.

Forum: Open discussion with audience, panel, and moderator. A meeting or part of a meeting set aside for an open discussion by recognized participants on subjects of public interest.

Forward Contract: An agreement guaranteeing a specific price for a product or service at a given future date. May also guarantee a specific rate of exchange when foreign currency is used.

Foul Bill of Lading: A receipt for goods issued by a carrier with an indication that the goods were damaged when received. See CLEAN BILL OF LADING.

Four-Hour Call: Minimum work period for which union labour must be paid (generally, a minimum call is one hour). Not to be confused with minimum charges to exhibitors applied by contractors who service events.

Freight: Properties, products, and other materials that are transported via ships, trains, trucks, or airplanes.

Freight Forwarder: A third-party logistics provider which handles export shipments for customers using common carriers.

Freight on Board (FOB): When something is purchased "FOB origin," the seller pays for transportation of the goods to the port of shipment, plus loading costs, while the buyer pays the cost of marine freight transport, insurance, unloading, and transportation from the arrival port to the final destination.

French Service - Banquet Style: A style of food service. In this pattern of service platters of food are composed in the kitchen. Each food item is then served from the guest's left by the server from the platters to individual plates.

Fresnel: A type of soft beam-focusing spotlight.

Fresnel Lens: Lens which produces a soft edged beam of light. Theatrical fixture with adjustable lens 150 W through 1500 W.

Front Projection: Projection of an image onto the front surface of a light reflecting screen from a projector placed above, within or behind the audience.

Front-of-House (FOH) **Audio Engineer:** A technician who manages audio equipment for an event and typically operates in the middle or back few rows of the seating area.

Full American Plan (FAP): See AMERICAN PLAN (AP).

Function: Any of a group of related organised occasions that contribute to a larger event.

Function Sheet: See BANQUET EVENT ORDER (BEO).

Gala Dinner: Primary social function of an event, usually in the evening, including entertainment or speeches after a formal meal.

Gamification: Application of game mechanics to engage event attendees; often used as a component of training and development via mobile event apps.

Ganging Menus: When two or more groups in a facility have the same menu.

Gate Show: Exhibition open to the public usually requiring an entrance fee. See CONSUMER SHOW. See also PUBLIC SHOW. Compare with TRADE SHOW.

Gel: Theatrical colour filter used in conjunction with theatrical projection fixtures and spotlights.

General Agreement on Tariffs and Trade (GATT): A multilateral treaty aimed at reducing trade barriers between the signatory countries and promoting trade through tariff concessions.

General Assembly: General and formal meeting of an organisation or company attended by a specified proportion at least of its members for the purpose of deciding legislative direction, policy matters, the election of internal committees and approval of financial matters. An assembly generally observes certain fixed rules of procedure.

General Liability Insurance: An insurance policy that provides protection against claims involving bodily injury and property damage to third parties.

General Service Contractor (GSC): An organisation that provides event management and exhibitors with a wide range of services, sometimes including, but not limited to, distributing the exhibitor manual, installation and dismantle, creating and hanging signage and banners, laying carpet, material handling, and providing booth/stand furniture. Also called OFFICIAL SERVICE CONTRACTOR.

General Session: A meeting open to all those in attendance at a event. See PLENARY SESSION.

Geofencing: A system for defining locations, such as an exhibit hall, using global positioning system (GPS) or radio frequency identification (RFID) technology.

Glass Beaded Screen: Screen whose surface is covered with tiny glass beads which reflect a bright image back toward the audience, but have a narrow viewing angle.

Global Reporting Initiative Event Organisers Sector Supplement (GRI EOSS): An international protocol for reporting on sustainable events.

Gobo: A pre-cut, etched pattern fabricated from metal or glass that fits in a lighting instrument to form projected light into a shape (logo, graphic, scenery, etc).

Goods and Services Tax (GST): Fee imposed on the sale of goods and services.

Gooseneck Light: Small (75 to 150 watt) spot light with flexible stem.

Gratuity: A payment that is given to service staff to signify good service. Depending on custom, local laws, and business practices, the payment may be added to the final bill automatically, based on a percentage of total charges.

Green Meeting Industry Council (GMIC): GMIC is a member of the Convention Industry Council.

Green Room: Room, stocked with refreshments, for artists, featured speakers and entourage to prepare, meet guests and media representatives.

Greenwashing: The practice of claiming or sharing false or misleading information in order to present an environmentally responsible image.

Gross Square Feet/Metres: 1) Total amount of available function space in exhibit hall or other facility. **2)** Total amount of space used for a specific show or event. See NET SQUARE FEET/MetreS (NSF/NSM).

Gross Weight: The full weight of a shipment, including goods and packaging. See TARE WEIGHT, ACTUAL WEIGHT.

Group Rate: Confirmed rate extended to attendees booking their sleeping room accommodations as part of a group room block.

Guarantee: A promise of commitment to provide a minimum amount of sleeping rooms, food and beverage (F&B), or other revenues. Usually there is financial liability if the commitment is not met.

Guaranteed Reservation: Pre-paid reservation held until agreed arrival time, or check-out time the next day, whichever occurs first. Guest is responsible for payment if reservation is not cancelled.

Guest Programme: Educational and/or social events or tours planned for spouses and guests of official event participants.

Halal: Food prepared according to Islamic dietary laws.

Half Moon Set-Up: A seating arrangement in which 60-, 66- or 72-inch (152-, 168- and 183-centimetre) diameter rounds have seats on two-thirds to three-quarters of the table and no seats with their backs to the speaker. Used for banquet-to-meeting or meeting-to-banquet quick set. See CRESCENT-ROUND SET-UP.

Hand Carry: Items that an exhibitor is allowed to carry unaided into a event facility without being charged.

Hand Service: One server is assigned for each two guests. Servers wear white gloves. When serving, they stand behind their guests holding two composed plates. When the signal is given, all guests are served at the same time.

Hard Close: The predetermined time when a bar is closed at an event and the servers are prohibited from dispensing alchoholic beverages.

Head Count: Actual number of people attending a function. See AUDIENCE COUNT. See also COVERS.

Headquarters: Facility, as the centre of operations, where registration, general sessions, and conference staff office are located.

Healthcare Convention and Exhibitors Association (HCEA): HCEA is a member of the Convention Industry Council.

Herringbone Set-Up: Seating arrangement in which chairs are arranged in rows slanted in a V shape and separated by a centre aisle. They face the head table or speaker. See CHEVRON SET-UP. See also V-SHAPE SET-UP.

High Boy: Small round table, 15- 30 inches in diameter (38- 76 centimetres) and 42 inches in height (107 centimetres) used for cocktail type parties.

High Season: Period when the demand for a supplier's product or service is highest. Prices generally increase in high season. Also called PEAK SEASON. Compare with LOW SEASON.

Hold Harmless: An indemnity clause that provides that both parties agree to defend and/or compensate the other party for asserted claims against, or liability damages incurred by, the other party due to the acts or omissions of the first party.

Hollow Circle Set-Up: Seating arrangement of tables and/or chairs all facing each other in a single circle.

Hollow Square Set-Up: Seating arrangement of tables set in a square (or rectangle) with chairs placed around the outside of the table. Centre (inside) table is hollow.

Honorarium: Voluntary payment made for services where no fee is legally required.

Horizontal exhibition: An exhibition that appeals to representatives of one or more industries through many types of products and services on display.

Horseshoe Set-Up: Tables set up in rounded U-shape with chairs placed outside. Chairs inside if needed. See U-SHAPE SET-UP.

Hospitality Sales & Marketing Association International (HSMAI): HSMAI is a member of the Convention Industry Council.

Hospitality Suite: 1) Room or suite of rooms used to entertain guests for business purposes. **2)** An event in which refreshments are served and exhibitor personnel and visitors socialize.

Host Bar: Private room bar set up where guests do not pay for drinks. See OPEN BAR. See also SPONSORED BAR.

Host Committee: A group of people bringing specific expertise of the locality and facilities of a given area to the Organising Committee in planning the event programme.

Hosted Buyer Programme: A programme that offers complimentary travel, accommodation and registration for prequalified buyers to meet with suppliers during an exhibit.

Hotel Accommodation: Sleeping room(s) at a hotel and rooming arrangements; usually specifying the hotel classification in terms of its amenities, facilities, level of service and cost.

Hotel Reservation: An agreement between the hotel to provide a guest room on certain dates and rate and the guest who agrees to use the hotel on the specified dates at the agreed upon rate (and any other terms). Normally, a deposit of one night's stay is required to hold the reservation.

House Brand: Brand of wine or distilled spirits selected by a hotel or restaurant as their standard when no specific brand is specified.

House Count: Number of guests or sleeping rooms actually occupied on a particular night.

House Lights: Lighting of room separate from stage lighting.

Houseman: Service-staff member who handles function-room set up and tear down. See BANQUET SET-UP.

Housing Bureau: Organisation that provides reservation services for a group and its attendees.

Housing Report: Document detailing housing utilization (reservations, pickup, etc.).

Hybrid Meeting: A meeting that combines face to face and virtual aspects.

IATA #: Identification of an accredited agent with the International Air Transport Association (IATA).

Image Magnification: Technology by which presenter's image is projected onto a large screen, allowing large audiences to see details from the stage. Also called I-Mag.

In Conjunction With (ICW): An event or function that occurs because of, or at the same time/same facility as, another event.

In-House: An adjective used to define services which are performed within the company or organisation, rather than being subcontracted.

In-House Contractor: Contractor retained by a facility to be on-site and provide services as needed, sometimes on an exclusive basis. In some cases, planners are not required to use their services, but may be charged a surcharge or facility fee for bringing in an outside contractor for the same service. See EXCLUSIVE CONTRACTOR.

In-House System: 1) A sound system that is built in to a venue. **2)** A system of handling attendee registration by the event host organisation. 3) Handling lodging reservations within the contracted room block at a hotel.

Incidentals: Expenses other than room and tax, billed to a guest's account (e.g. phone, room service, etc.).

Inclusive: Price charged to clients that includes all applicable gratuities, service charges/ fees and taxes.

Inclusive Rate: 1) For lodging and accommodations, the amount charged for a room, usually including breakfast (or other meals), taxes and service charge. See FULL AMERICAN PLAN(FAP). See also MODIFIED AMERICAN PLAN (MAP). 2) For food and beverage or catering, a rate that includes taxes, gratuities and/ or service charges.

Indemnification Clause: A contract clause in which one party agrees to pay damages or claims that the other party may be required to pay to another. For example, if a hotel is sued by an attendee that is injured at an event due to the fault of the group, an indemnification clause might require the group to pay back the hotel. Some times the law requires one party to indemnify another even without a specific clause. See HOLD HARMLESS.

Independent Planner: A third-party contractor who plans meetings or events for the contracting organisation.

Independent Show Management Company: A contractor hired by an exhibitor to perform event services independent of event management-appointed contractors. See EXHIBITOR APPOINTED CONTRACTOR (EAC).

Indirect Costs: Also called overhead or administrative costs, these are expenses not directly related to the event. They can include salaries, rent, and building and equipment maintenance.

Indirect Spending: Additional spending occurring within other industries that provide goods and services to the "direct" industries involved in meetings activity. See DIRECT SPENDING, ECONOMIC IMPACT and INDUCED SPENDING.

Individual Pays Own (IPO): The individual pays for a specific drink or service request, rather than the event host.

Induced Spending: Occurs when employees in a host destination's travel industry and its suppliers spend their wages in the local economy. This chain of buying and selling among businesses and employees continues until the original direct spending leaks out of the local economy. See also DIRECT SPENDING, ECONOMIC IMPACT and INDIRECT SPENDING.

Informal Meeting: Informal gathering, not necessarily social.

Infringement: Use of floor space outside exclusive booth/stand area.

Inherently Flame Resistant: Material that is permanently flame resistant without chemical treatment.

Inline Booth/Stand: Exhibit space with exhibit booths on either side and back. See INSIDE BOOTH/STAND.

Inspection Trip: See FAMILIARIZATION TRIP (FAM TRIP). See also SITE INSPECTION.

Installation: Setting up exhibit booth/stand and materials according to instructions and drawings.

Installation & Dismantle (I&D): The set-up and teardown of exhibits.

Installer: Skilled labour used to set up displays at events. The union affiliation of the installer will vary based upon the locale and the facility in question.

Institute: In-depth instructional meeting providing intensive education on a particular subject.

Integrated Marketing: Marketing activities with a common focus on the marketplace or a customer segment. The execution of each individual piece of the integrated marketing plan is consistent with, and supportive of, each of the other pieces of the plan.

Intelligent Lighting: Lighting instruments that can be computer controlled to move light around the room, and project colour and patterns on screens, scenery, walls or floor.

Interactive Exhibits: Exhibits that engage visitors through direct interaction with display components, working models, simulations, or multi-sensory or multi-media elements.

Interactive Learning: Learning activities that involve hands-on, direct experience activity by the learners, and interaction between learners.

Interactive Response: A system which enables the audience to respond to prepared questions by means of a multifunction keypad, text messaging or other electronic systems. Responses are collected and tabulated by software and can be shared or displayed graphically.

Interactive Video: Video which allows the viewer to be involved in an active way with the information to be presented.

International Association of Conference Centres (IACC): IACC is a member of the Convention Industry Council.

International Association of Exhibitions and Events (IAEE): IAEE is a member of the Convention Industry Council. Formerly known as International Association for Exhibition Management (IAEM).

International Association of Professional Congress Organisers (IAPCO): IAPCO is a member of the Convention Industry Council.

International Association of Speakers Bureaus (IASB): IASB is a member of the Convention Industry Council.

International Association of Venue Managers (IAAM): IAVM is a member of the Convention Industry Council. Formerly known as International Association of Assembly Managers (IAAM).

International Congress and Convention Association (ICCA): ICCA is a member of the Convention Industry Council.

International Event: 1) An event that draws a national and international audience. Typically 15% or more of attendees reside outside of the host country. **2)** An event that draws an audience from 3 or more countries."

International Freight Forwarder: A third-party logistics provider that handles export shipments for customers using common carriers.

International Organisation for Standardization's 20121 Event Sustainability Management Systems (ISO 20121): A process-oriented management programme developed to define the systems needed in order to implement sustainable event practices.

International Special Events Society (ISES): ISIS is a member of the Convention Industry Council.

Internet Protocol (IP) **Address:** A numeric value unique to an individual computer or electronic device that identifies it on a network. The IP address is assigned by a network administrator, Internet Service Provider (ISP), or other network hardware.

Internet Service Provider (ISP): A service that provides access to the Internet.

Interpretation in Relay: Oral translation utilizing two interpreters. Because the first interpreter is not master of the second language, another makes the final interpretation to the audience. See CONSECUTIVE INTERPRETATION, SIMULTANEOUS INTERPRETATION, WHISPERED INTERPRETATION, WIRELESS INFRARED INTERPRETING SYSTEM.

Interpreter's Booth/Stand: A soundproof cubicle in which the interpreter works.

Interview: A moderator, on behalf of the audience, asks the presenter questions

Invited Paper: Paper or speech on a specific subject submitted or presented at the request of an event's organisers, typically for an academic conference.

Invited Speaker: A person who is invited to deliver a speech during the conference. Costs of travel, housing and appropriate appearance fees may be provided for in the conference budget. May be issued a letter of invitation to assist with international travel.

Island Booth/Stand: Booth/stand space with aisles on all four sides.

Island Exhibit: A display space that is exposed to aisles on all sides.

Jigging: Special dividers, sectioning and protective padding inside exhibit crates.

Joint Agreement: Union contract covering more than one employer and a union, more than one union and an employer, or a number of employees and a number of unions.

Junction Box: A distribution point for electrical power.

Junior Suite: A hotel room that features a separate living-sitting area (although not a separate room), in addition to the bedroom. Also called a MINI-SUITE.

Jurisdiction: 1) The jobs that may be performed by a specific labour union. **2)** The locality where a contractual dispute is decided. **3)** In law, the ability of a court to hear and decide a matter brought before it.

Jurisdictional Dispute: Conflict between unions concerning the right to control certain jobs in a particular trade or industry.

Keynote Address: Opening remarks or presentation at a meeting that sets the tone or theme of the event and motivates attendees.

Keynote Session: Keynote sessions are designed to bring everyone together and may include a high-profile speaker or panel presentation.

Keynote Speaker: Speaker whose presentation establishes the theme or tone of the event.

Keystone Effect: Distortion of a projected image whereby the image is wider on top and narrower on bottom. Keystone effect is caused when an image source is not perpendicular to the centre point of the screen or projection surface.

Kiosk: 1) Free-standing pavilion or light structure, often inside a facility, where printed or electronic information is available. **2)** A small enclosure for ticket sales, information, etc.

Knock Down (KD): Exhibit or display components requiring on-site assembly.

Kosher: Food prepared according to Jewish dietary laws and restrictions.

LCD Projector: See Liquid Crystal Display (LCD) Projector:

Liquid Crystal Display (LCD) Projector: A self-contained unit with a liquid crystal display (LCD) panel, light source and lens that works with computers for displaying video, images or data on a screen or other flat surface without any need for special software or complex setting up. Also known as a data projector or beamer.

Lead Retrieval: The process whereby exhibitors receive a potential customer's contact information in a standardized manner. A system for capturing and following-up on leads generated at an exhibition.

Lead Tracking: A manual or automated system used to conduct follow-up activities for sales prospects resulting from an event.

Learning Environment: The physiological, psychological, social/cultural, industry, nutritional, technological, physical, service, personnel, and evaluation factors surrounding the learning experience.

Lectern: A stand upon which a speaker may rest notes or books. May be "standing," which rests on the floor, or "table-top" which is placed on a table. Often confused with PODIUM.

Lecture: Informative and educational talk to an audience.

Leko: Type of adjustable spotlight used to light lecterns, signs and areas that need a tightly focused pool of light. See ELLIPSOIDAL SPOTLIGHT.

Lenticular Screen: Screen finish with a characteristic silver-coloured finish which has brighter reflective characteristics than a matte screen but with a wider viewing angle than a beaded screen.

Less Than Truckload (LTL): Transportation rates applicable when the quantity of freight is less than the volume of truckload minimum weight, between 151 and 20,000 lb (68 and 9,072 kg).

Letter of Agreement: Document outlining proposed services, space, or products which becomes binding upon signature by authorized representatives of both parties.

Letter of Credit (L/C): A document issued by a bank per instructions from a buyer of goods, authorizing the seller to draw a specified sum of money under specified terms. See CONFIRMED LETTER OF CREDIT.

Liability Clause: Part of a contract outlining conditions of liability.

Liability Disclaimer: Legal statement releasing the organisation from responsibility for any arrangements made by attendees with services listed by the organisation (e.g., child care).

Licensing Agreement: A right or permission granted by the owner of a property (tangible or intangible) to engage in some business or occupation or engage in some transaction, which would be unlawful without such right, or permission. A business arrangement in which the manufacturer of a product (or a firm with proprietary rights over certain technology, trademarks, etc.) grants permission to some other group or individual to manufacture that product (or make use of that proprietary material) in return for specified royalties or other payment. Many convention centre agreements are written as license agreements.

Light Bar: A bar with a light that hangs behind a header.

Light Box: Enclosure with lighting and translucent face of plastic or glass.

Lighting: 1) Service offered by electrical contractor for illumination. **2)** Booth/stand or hall illumination. **3)** Existing light provided by the venue for functionality and safety. **4)** Controlled application of the art of lighting to impact sales, achieve atmosphere and otherwise enhance the experience of the event.

Lighting Control Console: Desk-type housing, used to contain the controls required for adjusting production lighting. Also known as the MASTER CONTROL.

Lighting Director: Person who designs the lighting, directs placement of lighting equipment, and calls lighting cues on-site.

Lighting Grid: Structures used to support lights and electrical outlets.

Lighting Plot: A print showing the location and type of all lights used in a booth/stand, or in a meeting environment.

Lighting Truss: A construction of tubular steel or aluminum alloy onto which lighting instruments are hung and which is in turn suspended above the stage or exhibit.

Likert Scale: The scale is a measure of attitudes with a numbered point, through a neutral centre, to an opposite point.

Line of Sight: A line of vision from an observer's eye (such as an audience member) to a distant point (such as a stage).

Line-Array Speaker System: A loudspeaker system made of specific and usually identical loudspeakers configured in a vertical arrangement to create a highly directional sound beam intended for directional control over distance

Linear Display: Also "IN-LINE DISPLAY". Exhibit space that shares one or more borders with neighboring exhibits.

Liquid Crystal Display (LCD): Display composed of mobile crystals in liquid suspension which align themselves and polarize light in response to a small electric change. The crystals are manufactured in pockets within the display which correspond to areas of dark on light background.

Load In/Out: Scheduled times for crew to load and unload equipment.

Loading Dock: Area on premises where goods are received. Usually a raised area that back loading trucks can back up to and offload freight easily.

Lockout: 1) Refusal by a facility to allow guests access to their guest rooms. **2)** Labour action where employers refuse access to the facility by employees.

Loop: 1) Closed electric circuit. **2)** A continuously repeated segment of music, dialogue, or images.

Loop Fabric: Fabric to which Velcro® fastener fabric will adhere.

Low Season: Period when the demand for a supplier's product or service is lowest. Prices generally decrease in low season. Also called VALUE SEASON. Compare with HIGH SEASON.

Low Voltage: Term applied to currents of 24 volts or less. Must be transformed from normal 110 volt input. Useful in animation, lighted model, etc.

Low-Key Lighting: Lighting in which picture intensity produces limited bright areas.

Lowboy: A type of truck that can be adapted for picking up loads at ground level.

Mag-Stripe: Magnetic Stripe. A lead retrieval system using a magnetic strip on either the back of a paper badge or on plastic badges similar to credit cards.

Magnetic Key Systems: Means by which doors in hotels or other facilities are locked or unlocked. Usually, these are cards as opposed to actual keys. The system permits security staff members to know what key was used to enter the room and at what time.

Manager on Duty (MOD): Facility personnel in charge of operations and/or guest relations for a certain period of time.

Manifest: Final official listing of all passengers and/or cargo aboard a transportation vehicle or vessel.

Marine Insurance: Broadly, insurance covering loss or damage of goods at sea. Marine insurance will typically compensate the owner of merchandise for losses sustained from fire, shipwreck, piracy, and various other causes, but excludes losses which can be legally recovered from the carrier.

Mark: Taped or chalked symbol on studio or stage floors designating exact placement of props, actors or exhibits. Also called SPIKE MARK.

Market Segments: Categorization of people, organisations or businesses by professional discipline or primary areas of interest for the purposes of sales analysis or assignment.

Marketing Promotional Opportunities (MPO): Sponsorship of logoed items (e.g. tote bags).

Markup: Difference between the cost and the selling price of a given product. Difference between the net rate charged by a tour operator, hotel, or other supplier and the retail-selling price of the service. Generally a percentage of the net rate rather than a fixed amount, as in a 20 percent markup on the net.

Marshalling Yard: A holding area where trucks or buses check in and wait for instructions before delivering or picking up freight or passengers.

Mask: 1) Scenic drape used to obscure undesirable view from the audience or to protect or cover. **2)** An item used or worn to hide the face. **3)** Covering an item with masking tape.

Masking: 1) Scenic draping to obscure undesirable items, such as equipment storage, or unused areas from view. Also used for security purposes. **2)** Sound applied to an environment to provide privacy in open areas. The term "masking" refers to the so-called "cocktail-party effect" where certain conversations are hard to pick out because similar sounds mask them. The ear-brain can be fooled into not hearing certain sounds if other sounds at lower volume but sufficient complexity are simultaneously present. Pink noise is most often used to cause intentional masking; its spectrum is shaped or filtered and fed to loudspeakers hidden above an acoustical tile ceiling.

Masking Drapes: Drapes used to cover storage and other unsightly areas, unused areas or for security.

Master: Original copy of something, such as an audio or video recording or filmed production.

Master Account: A record of transactions during an event where the resulting balance is paid directly by the group. May include room, tax, incidentals, food and beverage, audiovisual equipment, décor, etc. Also called MASTER BILL.

Master Bill: See MASTER ACCOUNT.

Master Control: See LIGHTING CONTROL CONSOLE.

Master Key: One key that will open function and guest rooms.

Master Monitor: Video monitor which shows only the picture being aired.

Master of Ceremonies (MC)**:** Person who presides over the programme. Also called emcee.

Material Handling: Services performed by GENERAL SERVICE CONTRACTOR that includes delivery of exhibit materials from the dock to assigned space, removing empty crates, returning crates at the end of the event for re-crating, and delivering materials back to the dock for carrier loading. It is a two-way charge, incoming and outgoing. Sometimes referred to as DRAYAGE. MATERIAL HANDLING is the preferred term.

Matte: Lusterless surface.

Matte Screen: Screen having a flat or matte white finish which does not reflect as effectively as a glass-bead screen, but can be viewed from virtually all front angles.

Matte White: Type of non-shiny screen surface used for front projection. It is the least expensive type of screen.

Mbps: Megabits (millions of bits) per second. A rate of data transmission over a computer network.

Media Kit: Packet of information that is supplied to the press or other media; contains all the details of an event that are required to attract media attention and attendees, including speaker biographies, boilerplate copy, etc.

Mediation: Dispute resolution process in which the parties use a third party to assist them in reaching a compromise. The mediator may work with both sides together, or may act as "go between" in an attempt to move the sides toward agreement. The mediator may act informally, or be appointed by a judge or by agreement of the parties through an alternative dispute resolution organisation. Unlike arbitration, a mediator is not empowered to impose a decision on the parties.

Meet and Greet: 1) A function that has been arranged so that a celebrity/dignitary can be introduced to attendees. **2)** Service for meeting and greeting persons upon arrival in a city, usually at the airport, pier or rail station and assisting them with entrance formalities, collecting baggage and obtaining transportation. **3)** A social function that allows attendees to network in an informal setting.

Meeting: An event where the primary activity of the participants is to attend educational sessions, participate in discussions, social functions, or attend other organised events. There is no exhibit component . Compare with CONVENTION, EXHIBITION, TRADE SHOW, CONSUMER SHOW.

Meeting Design: The intentional shaping of a meeting's form and content to satisfy specific and purposeful goals.

Meeting Industry Network (MINT): On-line information network tracking historical and future site/booking information. MINT is provided by DMAI to its members.

Meeting Management Company: A company, representing another organisation, handling site selection, negotiations and turnkey support for an event.

Meeting Manager: See PLANNER.

Meeting Professionals International (MPI): MPI is a member of the Convention Industry Council.

Meeting Profile: A written report outlining statistics of previous events, anticipated use of all services, profile of attendees, hotel occupancy patterns, etc.

Meeting, Incentive, Conference/Congress and Exhibition (MICE): An internationally used term for the events industry.

Memorandum of Understanding (MOU): A document that describes a formal agreement between two or more parties.

Mic: See MICROPHONE.

Microphone (MIC): Instrument which converts sound into electrical signals for transmitting or recording. Commonly abbreviated as MIC.

Microphone, Omnidirectional: MICROPHONE that picks up sound from all directions.

Microphone, Unidirectional: MICROPHONE that picks up sound primarily from the direction in which it is pointed.

Minimum Call: Agreed upon minimum number of hours of work to be done by a worker under the labour agreement. In cases where the work to be done is shorter than the minimum call, the worker is guaranteed payment for the full minimum.

Mix: 1) Visual repetitive and/or alternating projection of two different slides on the screen used to add emphasis. **2)** (Sound) adjustment of each microphone for volume and sound quality.

Mixer: 1) Audio unit by which sound signals from all sources feed into one system; allows for dissimilar inputs (microphone and line) to be combined and controlled into one output. See SOUND BOARD. **2)** An informal get together to give members of a group an opportunity to meet one another.

Mixing: Combining audio or audio sources.

Mixing Board: See SOUND BOARD.

Mobile Event App: A programme that is operated on mobile phones or tablets and includes event information such as the schedule, speaker bios and may contain other features including social media integration and audience response systems and data analytics.

Model: 1) An object made in miniature representing something to be constructed. **2)** A person stationed in an exhibit to demonstrate a product, provide attraction to booth/stand or greet visitors.

Modem: Modulator-demodulator. Computer component that enables a computer to send and receive data over telephone or cable lines.

Moderator: Person who presides over panel discussions and forums.

Modified American Plan (MAP): A type of room rate that includes breakfast and one other meal (usually dinner). See DEMI-PENSION. See also AMERICAN PLAN, CONTINENTAL PLAN, EUROPEAN PLAN.

Modular Exhibit: An exhibit that uses standardized components (e.g., panels, frames) that can be assembled and reassembled in different configurations for different needs.

Modular Panels: Partition units (walls, doorframes, etc.) in standard sizes, used for building booths/stands in the sizes desired in that context.

Monitor: 1) Video or audio device used to maintain a reference on the sound or video that is being sent out to the audience. Audio feeds given to performers are also referred to as monitors but do not necessarily represent the sound sent to the audience. **2)** Event staff who observe sessions, report on problems and count attendance. Also called session monitor.

Mono: See MONOPHONIC.

Monochrome: Images reproduced in black and white or in varying shades of a single colour.

Monophonic (Mono): Sound from one source, such as a single loudspeaker or earphone. In most concert performances, this is the type of sound provided to the audience. See PA SYSTEM.

Montage: 1) Composite made by combining several separate video or still images. **2)** Rapid succession of images to illustrate an association of ideas.

Motion: Formal proposal to be discussed and voted on in a meeting.

Move-In: The act of installing an exhibit or equipment.

Move-In/Move-Out Dates: Dates set for installation/dismantling of an exhibition, a meeting, or other event.

Move-Out: Dates set for dismantling. Also called TEAR DOWN.

Multi-Channel: With two or more communication bands (receivers).

Multi-Screen: The use of two or more screens at the same time. Also called MULTIVISION.

Multi-Track Conference: A conference with parallel programme sessions where participants have the choice to follow one or the other track or to jump from one track to the other during the duration of the event.

Multimedia: Use of two or more audiovisual media in one presentation.

Multivision: See MULTI-SCREEN.

Music License: Control of the performance of musical compositions by the composers and authors through granting of a license to perform. Controlled by the copyright laws.

Music Licensing: The right granted by one party to let a another party use live or recorded music through special agreements and fee structures, often conducted with organisations that represent artists.

Mylar: Trade name for polyester sheeting, usually clear or decorative metallic reflective finish.

National Association of Catering and Events (NACE): NACE is a member of the Convention Industry Council.

National Coalition of Black Meeting Planners (NCBMP): NCBMP is a member of the Convention Industry Council.

National Speakers Association (NSA): NSA is a member of the Convention Industry Council.

Near Field Communication: Protocols that enable data transfer between wireless devices that are within very close proximity (less than 10 cm).

Net Monetary Benefits: Measure of an event's profit calculated as revenues minus expenses.

Net Rate: Non-commissionable rate.

Net Square Feet/Metres (NSF/NSM): Actual amount of salable space used by exhibit booths/stands which excludes aisles, lounges, registration areas, etc. See GROSS SQUARE FEET/MetreS (GSF OR GSM).

Net Weight: Weight of goods without the shipping container.

No-Show: 1) Reservation made, but not kept. **2)** Any person, group or exhibitor who fails to appear to claim a meal reservation, exhibit space or ordered service. **3)** Participant did not attend, nor cancel according to cancellation guidelines -- an exhibitor a hotel guest , a meeting attendee or a speaker/entertainer.

Non-Performance: To neglect to carry out an agreement.

Obstructed View: View of stage, from audience seating, which is blocked.

Occupancy Rate: 1) In hotel/motel industry, the percentage of total number of available sleeping rooms actually occupied. Derived by dividing the total number of rooms occupied during a given time period (night, week, year) by the total number of rooms available for occupancy during that same period. **2)** Measurement of building use, usually expressed as an annual percentage rate comparing potential facility capacity to actual usage.

Off-Premise Catering: Foods usually prepared in a central kitchen and transported for service to an off-site location.

Off-Line: 1) Non-route airline ticketing service. **2)** Computer application performed while not connected to a computer network.

Off-Season: See LOW SEASON.

Off-Site: A term that describes any function or activity that occurs away from the primary event facility. Examples of its use include "Off-Site Food & Beverage," "Off-Site Venue," etc. See OFF-PREMISE CATERING.

Offer: A promise, proposal or other expression of willingness to make and carry out a contract under proposed terms with another party which has the ability to accept it upon receiving it. Space and rent proposal from a facility. It may be in the form of a contract or license agreement.

Official Contractor: Organisation appointed by show management to provide services such as set-up and tear-down of exhibit booths and to oversee labour, material handling and loading dock procedures. Also known as GENERAL SERVICE CONTRACTOR.

Offstage: Not in view of the audience.

On Consumption: A term used in food and beverage that refers to the purchasing option based on the amount utilized by the group. The organisation pays for the food and beverage based on the actual food and beverage served.

On-Centre: Refers to measurement of space from the centre of a solid object (such as a column) to another point.

On-Demand: 1) The opposite of real-time. **2)** Audio and/or video programming available on a Web site after the completion of an event, providing this content so Web site visitors can listen or view at their discretion.

On-Line Registration: Registration made via the Web.

On-Site: A term that describes any function or activity that occurs at the primary event facility.

On-Site Management: Details that the event manager must supervise at the site of the event.

On-Site Registration: Process of signing up for an event on the day of, or at the site of, the event.

One Ten/Sixty: Common term describing normally available current in North American Continent. The full expression is 110 volt/60 cycle. Many European and South American areas use 220 volt/50 cycle power.

One-Sheet: A one-sheet piece of printed advertising. Often promoting a speaker's product or services.

Open Bar: Private room bar set up where guests do not pay for drinks. See HOST BAR. See also SPONSORED BAR.

Open Hours: Hours during which an exhibition, event registration or business is open.

Open Seating: 1) Guests can sit anywhere. **2)** Extra banquet tables are placed, but not fully set; these can be prepared quickly if there are more guests than expected.

Open Space Technology Session: Meeting format where the agenda is set by the participants upon arrival. A facilitator helps participants organise into conversation groups.

Open-Ended Incentive Programme: Incentive programme where the possible number of winners are not predetermined. See also CLOSED-ENDED INCENTIVE Programmes.

Opening Address: Formal speech given at the commencement of a meeting to welcome participants; usually given by an eminent person.

Opening Ceremony: The formal general session at the beginning of a congress or convention.

Opening Session: Meeting which begins a congress or convention and in which the principal agenda items are introduced. Typically includes a KEYNOTE SPEAKER or OPENING ADDRESS.

Operations: Performing the practical work of operating a programme. Usually involves the in-house control and handling of all phases of the services, both with suppliers and with clients.

Operations Manager: Individual in charge of performing the practical and detailed work of a programme. See OPERATIONS.

Opt-In Marketing: See PERMISSION MARKETING.

Optical Sound: Sound that is recorded by photographic means on film sound recorded on and subsequently played back from an optical or photographic soundtrack, as opposed to a magnetic soundtrack.

Option: 1) Space which is reserved but not yet contracted for an event. The right of first refusal to confirm a tentative space reservation if there is demand from another group. See TENTATIVE HOLD. **2)** Options - Activities other than those included in the formal agenda which are optional and often require the payment of an additional participation fee done at the guest's discretion.

Option Date: A prearranged date by which a hotel or facility will no longer hold tentative arrangements for a group. Also called TENTATIVE HOLD.

Optional Tour: A TOUR or side trip offered at a designated date, time and price, and is not included in the formal agenda.

Orchestra Pit: Sunken area in front of the stage used to accommodate the orchestra.

Order of Precedence: A system which ranks dignitaries according to international protocol for purposes of seating, honors or ceremonies.

Organiser: The entity or individual that produces an event.

Organising Secretariat: Staff providing administrative services to the organiser.

Organising Committee: A group of people who carry out the strategies and policies established for the organisation of an event held in their geographic area. See LOCAL HOST. See also EXECUTIVE COMMITTEE.

OT: 1) Overtime. **2)** On Truck or Railway.

Out Take: Taped or filmed scenes not used in the final production.

Outboarding: The practice of conducting an event related to an existing meeting but not approved by the event's host organisation.

Outbound Operator: A company that takes groups from a given city or country to another city or country.

Outbound Tour: Any tour that takes groups outside a given city or country to another city or country.

Outside Exhibit: Booth/stand located outdoors.

Outside Vendor: Supplier who is not directly associated with the facility.

Outsource: To subcontract a task or responsibility to a supplier to handle some aspect of an event, instead of using in-house staff.

Over-Set: Number of covers set over the guarantee. Paid for by the client only if actually consumed.

Over-the-Road (OTR)**:** Freight that is transported on the road and over public highways.

Overage: Surplus, excess, or extra.

Overbooked: See OVERSOLD.

Overflow: Attendees booked into other facilities after headquarters facilities are full.

Overhead Projector: Equipment which projects an image on a screen by passing light through a transparent slide or other transparency.

Overlay: 1) Clear acetate film used to separate different components of art work. **2)** Tissue sheet over artwork on which corrections or alterations are indicated. **3)** A panel mounted to another surface. **4)** A second, smaller tablecloth used for decorative purposes at banquets. See DOUBLE CLOTH.

Overnight Service: A type of airfreight service. Overnight does not necessarily mean 24-hour delivery as carriers deal in business days (usually, Monday - Friday). In addition, a shipment might not move until the following day, depending on the time of day it is picked up or loaded.

Overnight Stays: The total nights spent by an attendee at a housing facility before, during, and after an event.

Override: A commission over and above the normal base commission percentage.

Oversold: Condition where the number of confirmed reservations exceeds the number of seats on an aircraft or sleeping rooms in a hotel. Also called OVERBOOKED.

Overstay: A guest who stays at a housing facility (hotel, motel, etc.) one or more days longer than his or her scheduled departure date. Also called STAY OVER. Compare with UNEXPECTED DEPARTURE.

Overtime: Time worked by an employee outside of, or in addition to, regular working time or beyond the standard workweek.

Overtime (OT) **Labour:** Work performed in excess of the standard day or week and typically billed at a higher rate.

PA System: See PUBLIC ADDRESS SYSTEM.

Pacing: 1) A rate of activity such as the presentation of a meal or tour itinerary. **2)** The scheduling of activities within an itinerary or meeting programme to make for a realistic balance of travel time, educational programming, social events, tours, free time and rest. 3) Rate at which reservations are being made with respect to the percent of the total rooms booked measured at different time periods and compared to past events.

Package: 1) Hotel, conference centre, or tour arrangement components combined and sold at a single all-inclusive price. **2)** A single-fee booth/stand package offered by event management which might include booth/stand space, one electrical outlet, and basic furnishings.

Package Tour: A travel offering which provides, at an inclusive price, several travel components that a traveller would otherwise purchase separately.

Packager: 1) An individual or organisation that coordinates and promotes the development of a package tour and establishes operating procedures and guidelines for that tour. **2)** Company that organises speakers' demo tapes, press kits, etc. for a fee.

Packet: The unit of data sent across a packet-switching network. It contains a destination address.

Packing List: Description and quantity of items contained within a shipment.

Pad Wrap: Wrap needed for protection of goods that are shipped without additional crating. See PADDING.

Padded Van Shipment: Shipment, by moving van, of crated or uncrated goods such as large pieces of furniture or display material.

Padding: 1) Usually blanket protection for uncrated material. **2)** Additional material for comfort installed under carpeting in an exhibit booth

Paid Out: In-house facility form authorizing a cash disbursement to be charged to master account or individual guest.

Pallet: Wooden platform used to carry goods. See SKID.

Pallet Wrap: Process of wrapping loose items on a pallet with a transparent plastic wrapping.

Pan: Panorama. Sideways movement of a camera to film a wide scene.

Panel Discussion: Instructional technique using a group of people chosen to discuss a topic in the presence of an audience, or for a virtual event, such as a Webinar.

Panel Dolly: L-shaped dolly with wheels on both the vertical and horizontal sides. Used for moving display panels.

Panel System: A prefabricated exhibit composed of connected panels of various sizes and shapes.

Par Lamp: A lamp shaped like an automobile headlight that consists of a tungsten source housed in an enclosed lens, which produces a rectangular beam.

Parabolic Screen: Type of front projection screen surface which is rigid and allows only narrow angle viewing.

Parallax: An apparent change in the direction of an object, caused by a change in observational position, that provides a new line of sight.

Parallel Session: Session which has some correspondence or similarity of subject, and is simultaneous to another session.

Parcan: A 150 watt to 1000 watt lighting instrument that acts like a floodlight providing an even light over a specific area; frequently seen in polished aluminum version, hanging in large groups from a ground support or flying truss system.

Parlor: Hotel living room, usually with a hide-a-bed sofa, connected to an adjoining sleeping room.

Parlor Suite: A hotel suite containing a PARLOR connected to an adjoining sleeping room.

Participatory Learning: Occurs when the participants share knowledge, experience and work together to learn.

Partition: See AIR WALL.

Party Planner: A person or organisation that works with clients to design and implement private parties and other social events.

Pascal: The unit of pressure or stress in the International System of Units (SI). In the United States, PSI (Pounds per Square Inch) is used instead. See PSI.

Passenger Name Record (PNR): The PNR is a record created in a computer reservation system (CRS) / global distribution system (GDS) when a reservation is made for a traveller. The PNR includes a set of identifying code letters and numbers unique to a single reservation, and contains information about a traveller's itinerary It forms the basic unit of information from which travel management reports are compiled.

Pastry Cart: Selection of desserts on a rolling serving cart.

Patch: 1) To temporarily join wires or slides by overlapping. **2)** Plug-in connection between two lines.

Patch Bay: See PATCH PANEL.

Patch Panel: Plug and jack assembly permitting studio outlets to be temporarily connected to dimmer outlet circuits; also found in studio sound systems. Also called PATCH BAY.

Pattern of Event Dates: The dates during which an event can be conducted. May be designated by specific dates, days of the week, months, or seasons (winter, spring, etc.).

Pavilion: 1) A designated area within the event highlighting a special product category for marketing and exposure. **2)** A free standing structure a short distance away from the main building.

PAX: Abbreviation for passengers.

Payment Order: Written authorization for payment to be made.

Peak Night: Referring to the night during an event when most rooms are occupied by those in attendance.

Peak Season: See HIGH SEASON.

PechaKucha: This design format originated in Japan and refers to sessions that include a series of short presentations of 20 slides lasting 20 seconds each. Other similar formats include Ignite® Talks of 20 slides lasting 15 seconds each.

Pedestal: A floor support for an exhibit component.

Pending Registration: Incomplete registration where the fees, full payment or forms have not been received.

Peninsula: Two or more exhibit spaces back to back with an aisle on three sides. Also called END CAP.

Peninsula Booth/Stand: An exhibit with aisles on three sides.

Penthouse Suite: Guest rooms and connecting parlors located on the top floors of a facility.

Per Diem: Per day. Daily allowance for food, lodging and, in some cases, incidentals and ground transportation expenses.

Per Person: Goods or services priced and/or purchased according to the number of guests expected to attend the event.

Percent of the Gross: Type of payment involving a fixed percent of the gross income for that service. This type of agreement is often used by facilities as the rental.

Percent of the Net: Type of payment involving a fixed percent of the net income after costs of providing that service. This type of payment is often used in services provided by exclusive contractors within a facility.

Percentage of Change Formula: Formula used to establish the variability in cost for future facility services.

Performing Rights Societies: Societies whose purpose is to provide collective licensing for copyrighted music. Examples include ASCAP, BMI and SESAC.

Perimetre Booth/Stand: Exhibit space located on an outside wall. See BACKWALL BOOTH/STAND.

Perimetre Seating: Seating arrangement in which chairs are placed around the walls of a room. The chairs are often meant for spectators to observe an activity or event in the centre of the room.

Peripheral Block: A group of rooms reserved by a party outside of the Event Contracted Block (ECB) but is present in the city as a result of the Main Event (for example, some international tour groups). A peripheral block's consumed room nights should be credited to the Main Event's total room nights for historical tracking purposes. A peripheral block may be used to help offset attrition charges against the ECB. A peripheral block usually negotiates its own terms. See also EVENT-CONTRACTED BLOCK.

Perk: Payment, benefit, or privilege received in addition to regular income or salary.

Permanent Exhibit: A product display held on a long-term basis, i.e., museum exhibit, office exhibit, mart, showroom, etc.

Permanent Import: In case of sales, with payment of duties and value added tax (VAT), or in case of free distribution, disposable or consumables usually exempted from payment of duties and VAT depending on each country. Quantity and value exempted at discretion of customs authorities.

Permission (Opt-in) Marketing: An e-mail marketing campaign that only sends messages to users who have requested (or opted-in) to receive specific types of information. e-mail conference reminders and newsletters are examples of opt-in e-mail marketing campaigns based upon permission marketing.

Permit Card: Card granting temporary employment rights to a non-union member, issued by a union having a closed contract with an employer.

Personal Manager: Manager of individual artist or group of artists.

Pica: Unit to measure type line length and height. Approximately 1/6 inch (.43 centimetre).

Pick-Up: Number of facility guest rooms actually used out of a room block.

Pilaster: A rectangular column that usually projects about a third of its width from the wall to which it is attached.

Pillow Gift: An in-room amenity left in the evening while an event is underway, that the attendee will discover upon returning to the room. Can be gifts from sponsors, etc.

Pink Noise: Filtered white noise that exhibits a constant power in any band of frequencies of the same span percentage. Generated to test loudspeakers in a room as well as to "tune" a room for best audio reproduction. See WHITE NOISE.

Pipe & Drape: Light-weight aluminium tubing and drapery used to separate exhibit booths/stands, staging areas, and other similar locations.

Piracy: Actively seeking to recruit or divert event participants, primarily attendees and exhibitors, away from official room blocks and into other hotel bookings, using a range of techniques to approach event participants and gain their business. Also referred to as POACHING.

Place Card: Card placed on the banquet table, inscribed with the name of the person designated to sit at that place.

Place Setting: Another name for cover (a combination of cutlery/flatware, glassware, china and napery).

Planner: Person who oversees and arranges every aspect of an event. The planner can be an employee of the organisation or a third-party contractor.

Planning Matrix: A grid used to plan meeting formats and finalize subject areas, topics and assignments.

Planting: The use of trees and plants to enhance the appearance of an exhibit or a stage.

Plastic Laminate: Any one of several of the melamine plastics bonded to paneling for durability and appearance. Often used in exhibit construction.

Plated Buffet: Selection of preplated foods and entrees set on a buffet table. Can also be set on a roll-in cart.

Plated Service: Foods arranged on individual plates in the kitchen and then served to guests seated at a table. See AMERICAN SERVICE.

Plenary Session: General assembly for all participants. See also GENERAL SESSION.

Plug-In: An additional piece of software that extends the capabilities of a web browser or other programme by allowing the display of multimedia files or performance of additional functions.

Plus Plus: Addition of taxes and service charges to a price when not included, designated by + +.

Plus-One: Any component of a package tour that is not included in the package price, but may be purchased as an added feature or to extend the length of the package. Tour options are purchased at additional cost.

Poaching: See PIRACY.

Pocket Programme: A shortened printed version of the event programme giving basic information in a way which is easy to refer to and convenient to carry.

Podium: Raised platform where a speaker stands when delivering his or her remarks. Often confused with LECTERN. See also DAIS, RISER.

Point: 1) Measurement of type size. Twelve points equal one pica—approximately 1/6 inch (.43 centimetre). **2)** A city, town, village, or other community or area which is treated as a unit for the application of freight rates.

Point Source: Sound originating from a single source, or as if from a single source, and filling an entire space. This type of sound system is most often seen in a concert configuration, where the stage and sound system is at one end of the room and no additional sources of sound are used.

Point-of-Purchase: Display to show product, where sales can be made.

Point-to-Multipoint Videoconference: A videoconference from one location to multiple sites.

Pop-Up Exhibit: Lightweight display normally shipped in molded plastic crates. See PORTABLE EXHIBIT.

Port of Entry: Destination providing customs and immigration services.

Portable Exhibit: An exhibit that "pops-up" or a self-contained exhibit that is lightweight and easily set up.

Portal: 1) Entry, doorway. **2)** A Web site or service that offers a broad array of resources and services, such as e-mail, forums, search engines, and on-line shopping malls to attract and retain a large audience.

Porters: 1) Staff who carry luggage for guests using trains, planes, and hotels. **2)** Staff who perform cleaning duties.

Post As: Instructions to a facility indicating the exact way a specific function should be listed on the facility's reader board.

Post Conference: Any event which is arranged for the period immediately following the conference proper.

Post-Con Meeting: Meeting at the primary facility at which an event occurred just after it has ended. Attendees generally include the primary event organiser, representatives of the event organiser/host organisation, department heads at the facility, other facility staff as appropriate, and contractors. Compare with PRE-CON MEETING. See also POST-EVENT REPORT.

Post-Conference Registration: Registration for an activity or function which follows an event.

Post-Consumer Material: An end product that has completed its life cycle as a consumer item and would otherwise have been disposed of as solid waste. Post-consumer materials include recyclables collected in recycling programmes, such as office paper, cardboard, aluminum cans, plastics and metals.

Post-Event Report (PER): The industry preferred term for a report of the details and activities of an event. A collection of post event reports over time will provide a comprehensive history for an event.

Poster: Visual presentation of a specified size, presented on a flat sheet of paper or card, with details of a specific topic.

Poster Board: Soft or cork board panel, used for displaying copy and/or graphics. See ABSTRACT BOARD.

Poster Exhibition: Area with display of posters.

Poster Presentations: Informal sessions near poster exhibition to present and discuss contents of posters.

Poster Session: 1) Display of reports and papers, usually scientific, accompanied by authors or researchers. **2)** A session dedicated to the discussion of the posters shown inside the meeting area. When this discussion is not held in a special session, it can take place directly between the person presenting the poster and interested delegate(s).

POV Line: See PRIVATELY OWNED VEHICLE LINE

Power Bandwidth: Frequency range over which a power amplifier can produce at least half power (-3dB). This important specification is the actual indication of an amplifier's true power output capability, since many amplifiers are capable of much higher power outputs if frequency extremes such as those produced by music are ignored.

Power of Attorney: An instrument in writing whereby one person, as principal, appoints another as his/her agent and confers authority to perform certain specified acts or kinds of acts on behalf of the principal.

Power Response: Measure of a loudspeaker's output with reference to its electrical input. Power response includes the total sound energy radiated into the acoustic space around the loudspeaker rather than just on-axis. Flat power response would indicate that a loudspeaker is radiating equal energy into all angles at all frequencies.

Pre- or Post-Event Tour: Organised outing taking place before (Pre-) or after (Post-) an event for both attendees and accompanying persons.

Pre-Block: Assigning a specific guest room prior to the arrival of the guest.

Pre-Con Meeting: A meeting at the primary facility at which an event will take place just prior to the event beginning. Attendees generally include the primary event organiser, representatives of the event organiser/host organisation, department heads at the facility, other facility staff as appropriate, and contractors. Compare with POST-CON MEETING.

Pre-Function Space: Area adjacent to the main event location. Often used for receptions prior to a meal or coffee breaks during an event. See FOYER.

Pre-Opening: Period of time before a property's SOFT OPENING.

Pre-Pleated: Material permanently pleated, ready for installation.

Pre-Registration: 1) Registering in advance to attend an event. See ADVANCE REGISTRATION. **2)** At a facility, pre-assigned sleeping rooms available for occupancy.

Pre-Registration List: Computer generated list of names pre-registered with a group.

Pre-Sales: Items such as books, tapes, videos, etc. sold to a client in advance of an event versus items sold on-site.

Pre-Set Service: Placing plated foods on banquet tables prior to seating guests.

Prefab: Pre-built exhibit ready for installation.

Preferred Carrier: Carriers that have alliances with exposition service firms and general service contractors. They receive preferential treatment.

Preliminary Announcement: The first announcement that an event will take place, giving the dates, location and theme. See also FIRST ANNOUNCEMENT.

Preliminary Draft: First draft. The first version of a paper or document which is subject to further amendment.

Preliminary Programme: The first public draft of an event's schedule giving details of ancillary activities confirmed at the time of release and usually containing event registration information.

Premium Beer: Brands of domestic or imported beer sold at a higher price point than other brands.

Premium Brand: Brands of spirits (hard liquor), beer and wine sold at a higher price point than other brands.

Premium Pay: Extra pay over the regular wage rate for work performed outside or beyond the regular working hours, for work on Saturday, Sunday or holidays, for night shift work, for hazardous, dirty or unpleasant work, and for production in excess of established standards.

Prep Area: Space used for food production and service not visible to guests.

Preplated Items: Food placed on plates in the kitchen prior to being served.

Presenter: Person explaining a given topic in an informational session.

Press Clipping/Cutting: Article, or portion of an article, cut from a publication.

Press Conference: A meeting or interview held to make an annoucement and communicate information to media representatives.

Press Office: Agency that collects and distributes information to the news media.

Press Officer: The chief public relations contact with the press/media for an organisation.

Press Room: A room where members of the media may obtain exhibitor press kits, conduct interviews, or relax. Larger press rooms offer computers, Internet access, and office equipment for use by the press in filing their stories.

Pressure Zone Microphone (PZM): This type of microphone can be placed on a large surface such as a table, floor, wall, or lectern. It picks up sound from entire room and is often recommended for conferences, group discussions, interviews, lectures, and recordings. Also called a boundary microphone.

Priority Point System: System of assigning points to exhibiting companies to determine the order in which firms will be allowed to select booth/stand space first for the next event. Also called Priority Rating System.

Privately Owned Vehicle (POV): The POV is a vehicle, such as a passenger car or van, that is owned or leased by an individual, as distinguished from trucks, tractor-trailers and other over-the-road vehicles that are owned or leased by a company.

Privately Owned Vehicle Line (POV Line): Special loading dock reserved for POVs where material is unloaded at prevailing material handling rates.

Pro Forma: Financial forms (invoices, profit and loss statements, balance sheets, etc.) based on future expectations; provided or made in advance to describe items or projections.

Pro Forma Invoice: 1) An invoice provided by a supplier prior to the shipment of merchandise, informing the buyer of the kinds and quantities of goods to be sent, their value, and important specifications (weight, size, etc.) **2)** A packing list on which a shipper describes what is being shipped including the quantity, the value, the weight, and dimensions.

Pro Number: Shipment number designated by the common carrier to a single shipment, used in all cases where the shipment must be referenced and used to organise and track the progress of each shipment.

Proceedings: Published volume transcribing the full conference sessions, which may or may not include details of the discussion.

Procession: Group of individuals moving in an orderly, often ceremonial manner.

Producer: Person or company responsible for the production of something; usually used in reference to a theatrical producer, event producer or an exhibit producer.

Production Company: A company that presents special effects and theatrical acts. This type of company may contract to put on an entire event or only parts of one. They sometimes hire speakers as part of their contract.

Productivity Tickets: Complimentary tickets awarded by the official airline after the event according to the number of attendees who used the airline.

Professional Congress Organiser (PCO): Companies or individuals specializing in event planning on behalf of a client organisation.

Professional Convention Management Association (PCMA): PCMA is a member of the Convention Industry Council.

Professional Speaker: A speaker who is paid a fee for performances and makes a living from presenting information to various organisations.

Programme: Schedule of events, giving details of times and places.

Programme Book: Printed schedule of events, location of function rooms, and other pertinent information.

Programme Design: Structure of event programme elements to achieve specific goals and objectives.

Programme Development: Planning that takes place before an event regarding its specific content and fabric.

Prohibited Cargo: Goods restricted by international convention. Also refers to drugs, weapons and ammunitions.

Projection Booth: Platform or area from which audiovisual presentations are controlled.

Projection Distance: Measurement from the projector to the screen.

Projection Screen: Surface on which images are displayed.

Projector: An apparatus for projecting an image on a screen.

Promotion: A media campaign, normally consisting of a series of public notices and advertising activities, aimed at ensuring maximum attendance by focusing attention on an event.

Promotional Fares: Reduced fares for travel to particular cities. The number of seats sold at the reduced fare is limited and, therefore, early booking is critical. These tickets also carry many restrictions.

Proof: 1) Final copy for approval before printing. See BLUELINE. **2)** To correct before final printing. **3)** Standard measure of alcoholic strength; e.g., 100 proof = 50 percent alcohol content.

Proof of Citizenship: 1) A document, necessary for obtaining a passport. **2)** A passport or other document that establishes ones' nationality to the satisfaction of a foreign government.

Proofing: Checking preliminary printed materials for errors before the final printing.

Property: 1) Establishment such as a hotel, motel, inn, resort, conference centre, or event facility. **2)** Something (e.g. an interest, money, or land) that is owned or possessed.

Proposal: 1) Plan put forth for consideration or acceptance. **2)** Communication sent by a supplier to a potential customer detailing the supplier's offerings and prices.

Props: 1) Stage furniture, set dressing. **2)** Articles used by actors, entertainers, or speakers.

Proscenium Arch: The visible opening that frames a stage (usually theatrical).

Prospect: A potential attendee, guest, buyer or exhibitor.

Prospectus: The document (printed or on-line) that promotes the chief features and benefits of a product or service to prospects.

Protocol: 1) Customs and regulations dealing with diplomatic formality, precedence, and etiquette. **2)** A formal description of message formats and the rules two computers must follow to exchange messages.

Protocol & Diplomacy International - Protocol Officers Association (PDI-POA): PDI-POA is a member of the Convention Industry Council.

Public Address System: Audio and/or visual system to convey messages to participants during an event. Often referred to as a PA SYSTEM.

Public Seminar: A seminar that is open to the public. Usually, tickets are sold to individuals.

Public Show: Exhibition that is open to the public, usually requiring an entrance fee. See EXHIBITION. See also GATE SHOW, CONSUMER SHOW. Compare with TRADE SHOW.

Public Space: Space in a facility that is open to the general public and may be available for private use.

Publicity: Gaining public visibility for an event (pre, during or post) via the media.

Pyrotechnics: Fireworks display.

Q&A: See QUESTION AND ANSWER PERIOD.

Quad Box: Four electrical outlets in one box, which should be grounded.

Quad/Quadruple: 1) Four-channel audio tape recording system. **2)** Room with two or more beds for four persons.

Qualifying: The act of determining a person's authority or financial ability to purchase a product or service or perform a specific function.

Qualitative Data: Descriptive information that is a record of what is observed, presented in narrative by the respondent. Also referred to as "soft data."

Quantitative Data: Information that is represented numerically so you can assign ranks or scores, or determine averages and frequencies. Also called "hard data."

Quarter-Round: Wedge shaped table with one rounded edge.

Question and Answer Period: Time immediately following a presentation for the audience to ask questions to the presenter. Often abbreviated as Q&A.

Questionnaire: a set of questions used to gather information.

Quick Set: Function room set-up that saves room turnover time, limits the number of event rooms required, and avoids additional charges for changing room set-ups.

Quick-Change Booth: Enclosed or draped area, close to the stage, for costume changes.

Rack Rate: Facility's standard, pre-established guest room rates.

Rail: Low drape divider between exhibit booths/stands, also known as a SIDE RAIL.

Rain Date: An alternate event date contracted to use in case of inclement weather.

Rally: Gathering to promote enthusiasm and excitement.

Ramp Session: Session added on to the end of the day's programme, usually after dinner, to accommodate extra papers or an extra plenary lecture.

Random Sample: A sample of a statistical population in which all members of the population have an equal probability of being selected and which is used as an unbiased representation of the population.

Rap Sessions: Informal sessions with no specific agenda.

Rapporteur: Person appointed to note and record the proceedings of sessions and to write summaries of the paper(s) presented for a final summation session. See REPORTER.

Rate of Exchange: The rate at which the unit of one currency may be exchanged for the unit of another currency.

Reader Board: At a facility, a listing, either printed or on a video screen, of the day's events including times and locations.

Real-Time: When on-line activities take place at a designated time, they are referred to as real-time events. A Webcast of a keynote presenter that can be watched live over the Internet is an example of a real-time event.

Rear Projection: Image presentation where the screen is between the viewer and the projector. Often used with a FRONT PROJECTION which is translucent to images being projected from the rear and can be viewed from the front.

Reasonable Accommodation: Any provision that aids the participation of a person with a disability, as long as it does not create a hazard to others, a major disruption in business or an undue financial or administrative burden.

Receiving Fee: 1) Fee charged by a venue for handling delivered packages; **2)** Fee charged in some countries by a government to officially recognize an event.

Receiving Line: Dignitaries, host, sponsor, and guest of honor lined up to greet guests.

Reception: Social function where beverages and light foods are served. Foods may be presented on small buffet tables or passed by servers. May precede a meal function.

Reception Desk: Desk or defined area where guests are received at a hotel, motel or inn.

Record Locator: An identifying number for the Passenger Name Record (PNR) in a file or record. See also PASSENGER NAME RECORD.

Red Eye Flight: A scheduled flight that departs late at night and arrives in the morning.

Referral Child Care: When an event host organisation publishes a list of child care service providers available. Attendees then make their own arrangements with these services.

Reflection: Sound or light energy which returns from a surface when struck. The amount and angle of reflection depends on the type and size of the reflecting surface and the frequency (wavelength) of the energy.

Refraction: The change of direction of a light ray passing from one medium to another of different density.

Refresh: To clean function space after specific functions, or during break periods. Usually involves refilling water pitchers, removing soiled articles, changing glassware, and performing other light housekeeping chores.

Refreshment Break: Time between meeting sessions. May include coffee, soft drinks, and/or food items. Some are planned around a theme.

Refreshments: Items of food and drink consumed between main meals; usually taken during breaks between meetings. See BREAK.

Refundable Deposit: A deposit made to a venue or supplier that may be returned under certain conditions agreed to by the venue/supplier.

Regional Event: An event targeted to attendees from a specific geographical area. May be a stand-alone event, or a regional version of a national event. Typically 60% of attendees reside within a 400 mile (640 km) radius of the event city.

Regional Exclusivity: A speakers bureau's/agency's exclusivity is limited to a particular region or territory.

Regional Security Officer: RSO. Consular official charged with the security of his/her country's nationals while traveling in his region.

Registrant: Individual who has submitted a registration form and attends an event.

Registrar: Individual responsible for handling registrations.

Registration: 1) Process by which an individual indicates his/her intent to attend a conference or stay at a property. **2)** A method of booking and payment. **3)** The process of recording data about an attendee (or exhibitor), sending a confirmation and creating a badge used on-site.

Registration Area: Designated area where event registration takes place.

Registration Card: Signature form used by facility when registering a guest.

Registration Data: Information about an attendee that is gathered as part of the registration process (occupation, fee category, etc).

Registration Desk: Desk or defined area where event attendees register for an event on-site or retrieve registration materials if they have pre-registered.

Registration Fee: Amount payable for attendance at a conference; may vary according to level of participation or type of membership.

Registration Form: Form used by an event attendee to sign up to attend an event. It is used to collect important information about the attendee and his/her intended participation in the event.

Relay Interpreting: Oral translation whereby an interpreter does not translate directly, but interprets the translation of a colleague, usually because s/he is not qualified to work directly from the original language.

Release: 1) Signed form giving permission to use a person's name, picture, or statement (often in an advertisement). **2)** Form signed by presenter allowing recording of presentation. **3)** Document provided by management to permit removal of goods from exhibition during event hours. **4)** To release space, as in returning unsold air or hotel reservations to the supplier that originally allotted them.

Release Date: See CUT-OFF DATE.

Released Value: 1) Limit of a carrier's liability. **2)** Stated value of a shipment when released to the carrier. If shipper declares a higher value than the per-pound limit, shipping costs will increase.

Religious Conference Management Association (RCMA): RCMA is a member of the Convention Industry Council.

Rental Booth/Stand: Complete booth/stand package offered to exhibitors on a rental basis.

Rental Charges: Cost of hiring a piece of equipment or function space for a specified period of time.

Rental Contract: Contract stating terms and conditions for rental of exhibition venue or for individual booth/stand within a venue.

Repeat Engagement/Booking: When a speaker does a second or subsequent booking for the same client.

Reporter: 1) Person appointed to note and record the proceedings of sessions and to write summaries of the paper(s) presented for a final summation session. **2)** Person who reports on an event for the media (TV, radio, print, Web sites, etc.).

Reporting Pay: Guaranteed payment to employees who report or show up ready for work at their usual time and find no work to do.

Request for Proposals (RFP): A document that stipulates what services the organisation wants from an outside contractor and requests a bid to perform such services.

Reservation: 1) An arrangement to have a sleeping room (at a hotel or other housing facility) held for one's use. **2)** Process by which an individual or group secures space at a facility.

Reservation Centre: Telephone or computerized reservation sales office.

Reservation Form: Form used by event organiser, housing bureau or lodging facility to register guests for sleeping rooms.

Reservation Method: Manner by which sleeping room reservations are to be made for attendees of a specific event (i.e., individually, via master list, etc.).

Reservation Request: A communication by which a guest indicates sleeping room requirements; these are forwarded to the hotel to secure a reservation.

Reservation Review Date: Designated day when the facility will release a block of sleeping rooms to the general public. See CUT-OFF DATE.

Resolution: 1) Ability of a projection system to distinguish and reproduce fine detail. **2)** Motion put forward for a joint decision; usually has the force of a legislative decision.

Resort: 1) Regions associated with recreation and leisure, such as the mountains, seashore, or natural or man-made attractions. **2)** A resort hotel offers or is located near facilities for sports and recreational activities such as tennis, swimming, sailing, etc.

Resort Casual: Attire for warm destinations, including mid- to knee-length shorts; collarless or golf shirts; khakis and sandals. Women may wear linen sheaths, casual skirts or sundresses.

Resort Conference Centre: A conference facility with at least one major amenity, such as golf or tennis.

Restricted Dialing: The ability to control telephone access often by excluding specific country or area codes and certain types of calls. This is often put in place for event rooms and show floor locations.

Résumé: See EVENT SPECIFICATIONS GUIDE.

Retention Rate: 1) The percentage of exhibitors or attendees that return to an event from one year to the next. **2)** The percentage of an organisation's membership or company's employees that remain with the organisation or company from one year to another.

Return on Investment (ROI): A financial ratio indicating the degree of profitability. Calculated as NET MONETARY BENEFITS / Meeting Costs x 100. Meeting costs may also be referred to as expenses.

Return on Objectives (ROO): Measurement of the benefit received for participating at an event based on pre-set objectives for success.

Revenue Management System: A sophisticated computer based pricing system that vendors use to adjust prices based on anticipated demand. Also referred to as Yield Management.

Reverberation: Sound which appears to echo and re-echo in weaker and weaker levels. Also called Reverb.

Revenue Per Available Room (RevPAR): A performance measurement commonly used in the hotel industry. It is calculated by dividing a hotel's net rooms revenue by the total number of available rooms, or by multiplying a hotel's average daily room rate (ADR) by its occupancy. Commonly referred to as RevPAR.

Reviewing Stands: Elevated platforms accommodating not more than 50 persons. Seating facilities, if provided, are normally in the nature of loose chairs. Stands accommodating more than 50 persons shall be regulated as grandstands.

RevPAR: See REVENUE PER AVAILABLE ROOM.

RFP Distribution Date: The date a Request for Proposals (RFP) is to be passed along if an event organiser is using an intermediary to distribute the RFP [i.e., If an event organiser sends an RFP to a Convention & Visitors Bureau (CVB), and wants the CVB to send the RFP to member hotels on a certain date, that date is the RFP Distribution Date.]. See also RFP PUBLISHED DATE.

RFP Published Date: The date a Request for Proposals (RFP) is released from an event organiser and is made public. See also RFP DISTRIBUTION DATE.

Rider: Additional clause in a contract stipulating special requirements.

Rigger: 1) Person responsible for machinery uncrating, unskidding, positioning, leveling, and reskidding. **2)** Skilled labour responsible for attaching signs, banners, truss, and other equipment to ceilings.

Rigging: 1) The process of attaching the cable on a crane to a piece of machinery or equipment. **2)** The process for hanging materials or signs. **3)** The structure to which hanging materials are attached.

Right of First Refusal: A courtesy a facility extends to a previously booked party to approve or disapprove a concurrent booking or to save uncontracted space for the previously booked party for programme growth.

Right to Work State: Where joining a union is not a condition of employment.

Rights Only: Selling only the rights to a sponsorship, with the buyer incurring expenses for production, installation and dismantle.

Riser: Raised platform. See DAIS. See also PODIUM.

Risk Management: The ongoing process of assessing the risks that may threaten attendees, the meeting or event itself, the organiser, or partner-suppliers, and applying the appropriate measures to manage the probability and consequences of such risks.

Risk Monies: Funds that an agency would not recoup should a tour not materialize, i.e., nonrefundable deposits to suppliers, promotional expenditures, printing expenses.

Room Audit: A process to identify attendees who occupy rooms outside the contracted room block for an event.

Room Block: Total number of sleeping rooms that are utilized and attributable to one event.

Room Capacity: Number of people that can function safely and comfortably in a room.

Room Deposit: Money that must be paid in advance in order for a hotel to guarantee to hold a function or sleeping room.

Room Nights: Number of sleeping rooms blocked or occupied multiplied by number of nights each room is reserved or occupied.

Room Occupancy Pattern: Number of single, double, triple, etc. rooms used.

Room Pick Up: The number of sleeping rooms actually used by event attendees and exhibitors.

Room Rate: The amount charged for the occupancy of a room.

Room Service: 1) Facility department which provides food and beverage service to guest rooms. **2)** Food and beverage provided to guest rooms (In Room Dining).

Room Set-Up: The physical arrangement of a room including the layout of tables, chairs, other furniture, and equipment.

Room Tax: See TRANSIENT OCCUPANCY TAX.

Room Turnover: Amount of time needed to tear down and reset a function room.

Room-Based Videoconferencing: Land-based system for videoconferencing designed to manage communication between one group of people, usually in a conference room setting, with another group or groups in similar settings elsewhere.

Room, Tax and Incidentals (RTI): RTI is an abbreviation often used in reference to charges at an hotel, motel, inn, bed and breakfast, etc.

Rooming List: A list, whether printed or electronic, by which an event organiser and/or their designates (e.g. a housing bureau) delivers multiple reservations to a hotel or other housing facility. Often the information contained in a rooming list is originally gathered through attendees' completed Housing Forms. See also HOUSING FORM.

Rostrum: Raised platform where a speaker stands when delivering his or her remarks. Same as PODIUM.

Round: Banquet table, usually 60 inches (152 centimetres) in diameter. Also available in 66- and 72-inch (168- and 183 centimetre) diametres. A "Round for 8" is a banquet table at which 8 place settings should be set. Another common configuration is a "Round for 10." Commonly, a 60-inch (152 cm) round is used to seat 8, a 66-inch (168 cm) round seats 9, and a 72-inch (183 cm) round seats 10.

Round Robin: Contest or tournament in which each participant is matched with every other participant.

Rounded Hollow Square: A HOLLOW SQUARE SET-UP with corners replace by SERPENTINE or QUARTER-ROUND tables.

Roundtable: A group of experts who meet on an equal basis to review and discuss specialized, professional matters, either in closed session or, more frequently, before an audience.

Route Manager: The person responsible for managing motor coach flow, routes, drivers, etc.

Row Booth/Stand: The booth/stand within a row of similar booths/stands with the front opening onto an aisle and with other booths/stands on either side.

Run-of-House (ROH): **1)** Rooms given at random according to availability when the reservations are made. **2)** Flat rate for which a hotel or motel agrees to offer any of its available rooms (with the exception of suites) to a group. Final assignment of rooms is at the discretion of the hotel. See FLAT RATE.

Run-Through: A complete rehearsal including all elements of the event production, such as presentations, performances, music or entertainment, lighting, audio-visual and technical aspects.

Runner: **1)** Long narrow carpet in a hallway, aisle, or on stage. **2)** Piece of portable or constructed staging that extends a main stage to form a runway. **3)** Main cord extending from a microphone to an amplifier. **4)** A piece of decorative cloth laid across a tablecloth or buffet table to add colour or texture or to enhance a theme.

Runway: Platform which extends from a stage into the audience area, often used for events such as fashion shows.

Russian Service: Banquet Russian: The food is fully prepared in the kitchen. All courses are served either from platters or an Escoffier dish. Tureens are used for soup and special bowls for salad. The server places the proper plate in front of the guest. After the plates are placed, the server returns with a tray of food and, moving counter-clockwise around the table, serves the food from the guest's left with the right hand. With this style of service, the server controls the amount served to each guest. See BUTLER SERVICE.

Saddle-Stitch Binding: Binding process using wire staples, thread, or wire.

Sampling: 1) A research method based upon selecting a portion of a population for study. **2)** A food and beverage tasting provided to prospective clients for the purpose of menu selection.

Satellite Meeting: See IN CONJUNCTION WITH.

Scattered Arrivals: A pattern of group arrivals that are separate from the main arrivals.

Schoolroom Perpendicular Set-Up: Variation of schoolroom set-up in which tables are perpendicular to the head table, and chairs are placed on both sides of the tables.

Schoolroom Set-Up: See CLASSROOM SET-UP.

Schoolroom V Set-Up: Seating arrangement where rows of tables and/or chairs are slanted in a V-shape facing a head table, stage or speaker. See CHEVRON SET-UP.

Scissor Lift: A mobile work platform that extends vertically on a scissor-like mechanism with no increase in the size of the machine's footprint.

Screen Left and Right: Directions given from audience perspective.

Screen/Audience Distance: Distance between the projection screen and the front row of the audience. Rear most audience member should be no more than 8 times the height of the screen in use.

Scrim: 1) Translucent material used to diffuse or soften light. **2)** Gauze-like theatrical curtains.

Season: Period of time when the demand for a certain supplier's product or service is high, low, or neither. See HIGH SEASON, LOW SEASON, SHOULDER SEASON.

Second Option: Second place on a waiting list. The organisation holding the second option for specific dates at a facility, for example, may book those dates only if the organisation holding the first option decides not to book within a certain period of time. See OPTION.

Second Tier City: A city where the space of the convention centre, the hotels, or the air lift, make the city more appropriate for smaller meetings and events.

Secondary Airport: An airport that is used as an alternative to a city's primary airport.

Secure Digital Certificate: An encrypted file that authenticates the source of financial data, usually for an on-line credit card transaction.

Security Cage: Portable wire enclosure used to lock up materials for safe storage.

Security Contractor: Company hired by exhibit or event management to keep individual exhibits and the entire event floor safe using guards, closed circuit T.V., etc.

Security Service: Service providing security arrangements, such as checking credentials, searching hand luggage, protecting equipment and patrolling congress and exhibition areas.

Segue: Transition between two audio passages or video segments.

Semi-Skilled Labour: Persons whose work is limited to a well-defined work routine; or work in which lapses of performance would not cause excessive damage to products or equipment.

Seminar: 1) Lecture and dialogue allowing participants to share experiences in a particular field under the guidance of an expert discussion leader. **2)** A meeting or series of meetings of a small group of specialists who have different skills but have a specific common interest and come together for training or learning purposes.

Serpentine: Curved, S-shaped tables that when placed together make a snake form.

Serpentine Queue: Line formation of people going to the same area; line feeds off into several different service stations.

Service Bar: A counter from which alcoholic beverages are served that is located outside of a function room, usually in an area not visible to guests.

Service Charge: 1) A mandatory and automatic amount added to food and beverage charges, usually used to defray the cost of labour and service equipment. Generally calculated as a percentage of charges. **2)** A fee charged to a client by a travel agent in addition to the commissions paid to him or her by his or her principals.

Service Contractor: Outside company used by clients to provide specific products or services (e.g. pipe and drape, exhibitor manuals, floor plans, dance floors or flags). See also GENERAL SERVICE CONTRACTOR.

Service Desk: Centralized on-site location for ordering or reconfirming services provided by general service contractor and specialty contractors.

Service Kit: See EXHIBITOR MANUAL.

SESAC: An organisation similar to ASCAP and BMI that licenses the use of copyrighted music for various artists. Formerly called the Society of European Stage Authors and Composers.

Set: 1) Performance area including props, equipment, backdrops, etc. **2)** Length of time musicians play before taking a break. **3)** Make preparations for a predetermined number of attendees.

Set Dressing: Props arranged to decorate the set. Also called TRIM PROPS.

Set For: The actual number of seats put in place (or to be put in place) for a function.

Set Light: Light which illuminates background behind the performers.

Set-Up: 1) Way in which a function room is arranged. **2)** Erecting displays, installation, or, articles in their assembled condition. **3)** Mixers, fruit, and glassware accompanying a liquor order.

Set-Up Drawings: The plans from which the exhibit components are assembled.

Set-Up Personnel: Exhibit or function room equipment installers.

Shell Scheme: European booth/stand system—usually includes raised floor, back and side walls, plus fascia.

Shimmer Curtain: Draping made of strips of coloured material that catch and reflect the light.

Shipper's Export Declaration: A form required for all shipments by the U.S. Treasury Department and prepared by a shipper, indicating the value, weight, destination, and other basic information about an export shipment.

Shipping Agent: Third-party hired to handle shipping goods to and from an event. Also called a shipper.

Shipping Manifest: An instrument in writing, signed by the captain of a ship that lists the individual shipments constituting the ship's cargo.

Shirring the Drape: Gathering drape along the rods to even out the folds and give each panel of drape equal spacing.

Shop Steward: Person designated by the union within a shop or unit to represent employees.

Shore Excursion: Land tours, usually available at ports of call, sold by cruise lines or tour operators to cruise passengers.

Shoulder: The beginning and ending days of a room block when fewer rooms are contracted.

Shoulder Season: Period when the demand for a supplier's product or service is neither high nor low. See HIGH SEASON and LOW SEASON.

Show: 1) Organised performance for entertainment. 2) An exhibition. See EXHIBITION.

Show Breaking: Time specified for the close of the exhibition and the start of dismantling.

Show Card: Material used for signs.

Show Daily: A newspaper (printed or electronicallly produced) published each day during the run of an event or conference. It includes articles about the exhibits and events and, often, advertising.

Show Directory: A listing, with booth/stand numbers, of all the exhibitors in an event and a map showing booth/stand locations.

Show Management: The company, group or organisation that manages an exhibition. See also EXHIBITION MANAGER; SHOW PRODUCER.

Show Manager: See EXHIBITION MANAGER.

Show Office: On-site event management office.

Show Organiser: See EXHIBITION MANAGER.

Show Producer: Company or individual who is responsible for all aspects of planning, promoting and producing an event. See EXHIBITION MANAGER. See also SHOW MANAGEMENT.

Show Rates: Rates established by event management, official service contractors and/or other official service providers, and published in the EXHIBITOR MANUAL.

Show Rules: The requirements and procedures prepared by event management for exhibitors and contractors at a given event

Show Within a Show: An event with its own name and focus that takes place within a larger, related event. See IN CONJUNCTION WITH.

Shuttle: A vehicle, usually a bus or van, contracted to transport event attendees between facilities during a certain time period.

Shuttle Service: Transportation for participants; usually by bus or van, provided on a continuous basis for a certain time period.

Side Fills: Speakers on stage right and stage left to project amplified sound to full stage area.

Side Rail: A low divider panel (usually 3 ft. or .9144 metres high) used to separate an exhibit space from an adjacent area.

Sight Acts: Performers who must be watched to be appreciated, such as mimes, jugglers, dancers, and acrobats.

Sightlines: The actual or virtual lines in the venue or on paper layout that describe what parts of a set or decorative object are visible from a given audience or guest point of view; used to determine what must be decoratively treated or masked (hidden).

Signed Exception: Delivery receipt, signed by the carrier, noting a damage or shortage.

Simple Random Sample: Method of sampling in which each member of the population has an equal chance of being included in the sample.

Simulation: Interactive instructional technique in which the learner has an opportunity to practice a new skill in a simulation, imitation or role-play of a real life situation.

Simultaneous Interpretation: Process of orally translating one language into another while the speaker is speaking. See CONSECUTIVE INTERPRETATION, INTERPRETATION IN RELAY, WHISPERED INTERPRETATION, WIRELESS INFRARED INTERPRETING SYSTEM.

Simultaneous Translation: Process of translating one language into another while the speaker is speaking. Same as SIMULTANEOUS INTERPRETATION.

Single: Sleeping room occupied by one person. The room may have one or more beds in it.

Single Camera: A video signal that captures a single camera angle for recording an event or show. Also referred to as an isolated (ISO) camera feed.

Site: 1) Venue, area, location, property or specific facility to be used for an event. See EVENT SITE, VENUE. **2)** A particular platform or location for loading or unloading at a place.

Site Inspection: In-person on-site review and evaluation of a venue or location for an event.

Site Selection: Choosing a venue or location for a meeting or event.

Six-by-Six Rule: See 6-by-6 Rule.

Skid: 1) Pallet. **2)** Wooden platform used to support machinery or a collection of objects for easier handling. **3)** Thick wood blocks attached to crates which allow forklift access for easier handling. **4)** Wood runners protecting the exterior of a shipping case.

Skirting: Pleated or ruffled draping used around with tables, risers or stages to conceal the area underneath.

SLA: Service Level Agreement. Usually an adjunct document to a vendor contract.

Sling: 1) A pre-made length of cable used for hanging exhibit materials or signs. **2)** A pre-made length of cable or a heavy-duty nylon strap used for rigging machinery to cranes or forklifts.

Slippage: Reduction in the number of rooms used from the original reserved block.

Small Group Learning Patterns: A learning activity that is dependent on the participation of a small group of people.

Smart Board®: An interactive presentation white board that interacts with a computer image. Your finger becomes the mouse.

Smart Form: A Web-based form that can be designed to guide the user through the process of completing the form and can alert the user to errors.

SMERF: Acronym for a category of event market segments including Socia/Sport, Military, Educational, Religious and Fraternal groups.

Social Event: 1) An event with the purpose of facilitating networking among attendees, **2)** Lifecycle celebration (e.g. a wedding, bar/bat mitzvah, anniversary, birthday, etc.).

Social Programme: Programme of organised functions, not directly related to the main educational subject of an event.

Society for Incentive Travel Excellence (SITE): SITE is a member of the Convention Industry Council. Formerly known as Society of Incentive Travel Executives.

Society of Government Meeting Professionals (SGMP): SGMP is a member of the Convention Industry Council.

Soffit: A lowered portion of a ceiling.

Soft Currency: A currency that cannot be traded outside its native country.

Soft Opening: Time when a property is open for business, prior to the grand opening. All services/facilities may not be complete or available.

Sole Relay Interpreter: Pivot Interpreter; only interpreter in the team assigned to an event who is able to translate out of a lesser used language and functions as a "relay" for the rest of the team in relation to that language.

Sommelier: A wine steward, expected to have an extensive knowledge of wines and their suitability with various dishes.

Sound Board: Console with separate channels to control volume and sound quality produced by each microphone.

Sound Check: Verification, often by the performer, that the sound system to be used for the performance is functioning satisfactorily. Usually this is one of the final steps of the move-in.

Sound Control Booth: Area from which technician operates sound system in a room.

Sound Effects: Artificially produced sounds for a theatrical effect.

Sound Mix: Procedure of combining independently recorded narration, music and/or sound effect to single master tape or film, while at the same time establishing tone, volume and balance between elements.

Sound Reinforcement: Use of electronic and electric equipment to amplify the natural sound produced by a performer or speaker.

Sound Wings: Risers on stage right and stage left for stacked sound equipment which allows storage space hidden from the audience's view.

Soundscape: Atmosphere created with the use of music and sound effects.

Source Language: Language from which a speech or document is translated or interpreted.

Southern African Association of the Conference Industry (SAACI): SAACI is a member of the Convention Industry Council.

Space Assignment: Booth/stand space assigned to exhibiting companies or meeting rooms assigned to event groups.

Space Draw/Selection: The process of assigning exhibit space for the next event based on the exhibitors' active involvement in the process.

Space Rate: Cost per square foot/metre for exhibit space.

Space Requirements: 1) Amount of space required in a venue for a meeting or event. **2)** Amount of stand/booth space required by individual exhibitors.

Space Reservation Form: Form or special request to use a particular space.

Speaker: 1) The presenter of a programme. Types of speakers include keynote, general session, seminar leader, trainer, workshop leader, and "change of pace" speakers such as humorists and entertainers. **2)** Device for sound output.

Speaker Platforms: Platforms on the right and left of stage used to elevate sound equipment.

Speaker Ready Room: Area set aside for speakers to meet, relax, test AV, or prepare prior to or between speeches.

Special Event: One time event staged for the purpose of celebration; a unique activity.

Special Event Tour: A TOUR designed around a particular event, e.g. Wimbledon or Mardi Gras.

Special Events Company: A company that produces events which include a variety of creative elements including décor, special effects, theatrical acts or other entertainment. They may produce stand-alone events or functions within a larger programme such as a gala dinner during a convention.

Special Handling: Applies to display shipments requiring extra labour, equipment, or time in delivery to booth/stand area.

Special Interest Tour: A TOUR designed to appeal to clients with a curiosity or a concern about a specific subject. Most special interest tours provide an expert tour guide and usually visit places and/or events of specific interest to the participants.

Special Needs: Any physical or mental consideration that requires accommodations to ensure an event's physical space, technologies, and food and beverage accommodates those individual needs. Special needs can include food allergies, mobility device access, signing interpreters, etc.

Special-Interest Group: Group travel programme designed for persons with common interests.

Spike Mark: Tape or chalk marks on studio or stage floors designating exact placement of props and actors. See also MARK..

Split Folio: This is when a guest has two folios, one for room and tax and the other for incidental charges. Most often used when the room and tax are going on the MASTER ACCOUNT, and the guest (often a speaker, VIP or staff) is responsible for incidental charges such as in-room dining.

Split Screen: Horizontally or vertically separated video pictures shown simultaneously.

Spokesperson: A designated representative who has the authority, knowledge, and credibility to speak and be interviewed by the media.

Sponsor: 1) Organisation(s) underwriting all or part of the costs of an event. **2)** An individual who assumed all or part of the financial responsibility for an event. **3)** A commercial entity that provides financial backing for an event, and, which in return, receives recognition, advertising, registrations, or other benefits. Sponsors may or may not participate in any of the profit from the event.

Sponsor Prospectus: Promotional materials sent to current and prospective event sponsors to encourage participation. It promotes the value of sponsoring and contains information about attendee demographics, event programme and sponsor benefits.

Sponsored Bar: Private room bar set up where guests do not pay for drinks. See OPEN BAR. See also HOST BAR.

Sponsorship: 1) Donated financial or material support, usually in exchange for recognition. **2)** Paid opportunity for entity or an exhibitor to increase its visibility at the event.

Spot Exchange: The exchange rate for foreign currency for immediate purchase/delivery.

Spot Time: Designated time for vehicle or staff to report to assignment.

Spotlight: Strong focused light thrown upon a particular person or object, such as on a stage.

Spotting: Placement of equipment in exact location in booth by using a forklift.

Square Set-Up: Seating arrangement in which double- or triple-wide tables are set up with chairs placed around all sides.

Stack: Buses assembled in one location convenient for passenger loading.

Stadium: Facility usually designed for football (soccer), American football, cricket, rugby or baseball as a primary function. May be domed or open-air. Sometimes difficult to distinguish from a large arena.

Stage: The portion of an auditorium or room that has been structured into a formal area for productions or presentations.

Stage Call: 1) Designated time and/or number of crew members required at stage for task assignments. **2)** Asking a celebrity or speaker to return to the stage after completing the presentation.

Stage Directions: Instructions in the script concerning movements and arrangements on the stage.

Stage Left and Right: Directions from the perspective of a person on stage. See AUDIENCE LEFT AND RIGHT. See also SCREEN LEFT AND RIGHT.

Stage Lighting: Illumination for the platform for performers, musicians, actors, or speakers

Stage Manager: Person responsible for running the event on stage.

Stage Master: Person at a venue in charge of stage facilities.

Stage Plot: Diagram, drawn to scale, indicating placement on stage of equipment, props, microphones, etc.

Stage Right and Left: Directions from the perspective of a person on stage. See AUDIENCE LEFT AND RIGHT. See also SCREEN LEFT AND RIGHT.

Stagehand: Union labour that handles spotlights, rigging, and scenery for theatrical productions. In some cities, they may also handle decorating tasks, such as hanging draperies at convention facilities.

Staging: 1) Design and placement of elements for events. **2)** Implementation of an event.

Staging Area: 1) A place for demonstration. **2)** In catering, an area for preparing service equipment and supplies. **3)** A preparation area, usually on premises, where suppliers review orders and organise items before delivering them to exhibit booths/stands. **4)** An area near the event site where buses wait to be dispatched.

Stakeholder: Person(s) who or organisation(s) that have an impact on the success of an event or are affected by the event.

Stakes: Pointed pegs used to secure the guy ropes of a tent in the ground. Wooden stakes are used for grass-covered earth, steel stakes are required when the ground is extremely hard, rocky or paved.

Stand: European term for booth or exhibit. See BOOTH.

Star Rating: A rating indicated by stars (usually 1–5), the highest number of stars indicating the best quality of services at a facility or restaurant. Used by leading travel publications.

State Travel Office: An official government agency or privately run, nonprofit organisation responsible for travel development and promotion of a state (or territory). Often, an office responsible for travel development is part of another department or agency of a state government such as commerce and economic development. State travel offices vary in sizes of staffs and budgets.

Statement of Account: Statement of income and expenses following the end of an event.

Station: A banquet server's assigned area. Also refers to the individual buffet tables located throughout a reception area, with each table offering one food item or representing one theme.

Stay Over: A guest who stays at a housing facility (hotel, motel, etc.) one or more days longer than his or her scheduled departure date. Also called OVERSTAY. Compare with UNEXPECTED DEPARTURE.

Steering Committee: Select group which sets policies and makes basic decisions relative to a group or an event.

Step-On-Guide: A freelance guide who comes aboard a motorcoach to give an informed overview of the city or attraction to be toured.

Storage Area: Space at a show set aside for storage of crates or materials.

Storyboard: Series of sketches or pictures which outline the subject to be developed.

Straight Time (ST) **Labour:** Labour performed and paid at standard rate for work during normal business hours as established by unions.

Strategic Meetings Management Programme (SMMP): A focused approach on increasing efficiency and reducing costs across the organisation for all of its events.

Strategic Relationships: An agreement between two or more enterprises to conduct specified business processes in a joint manner.

Streaming: The software that distributes audio and video from a central source, or media server, to recipients on their personal computers or mobile devices.

Streaming Media: A method for delivering audio and video over the Web. Streaming refers to the ability of Web site visitors to access multimedia content without having to download an entire file first.

Strike: **1)** Dismantle exhibits. **2)** To remove all scenery and props from the stage. **3)** Union walkout.

Strobe Light: Rapidly blinking, high-intensity light.

Structured Question: Prepared questions, usually eight or ten per one hour presentation, to be distributed in advance of the session to selected attendees. Following each presentation, attendees ask questions from the list.

Studio: Room with a couch or couches that convert to beds.

Style Sheet: A list of special spellings, terms and style points to be used consistently in publications related to an event, company or organisation.

Sub-Block: Any group of rooms that is classified or separated differently than the general attendee block within the Event-Contracted Block (ECB). See also EVENT-CONTRACTED BLOCK.

Subcommittee: A group of people, frequently including one or more members of the main committee, meeting outside of the main committee, with responsibilities for specific items.

Subcontractor: **1)** An individual or business, which contracts to perform part or all of the obligations of another's contract. **2)** Company retained by a contractor to provide services to exhibitors or event management; outsourcing.

Suburban Hotel: Hotel on the outskirts of a large city, which may or may not be near local attractions.

Subvention: Financial support provided by the host destination or government as an incentive to attract large congresses or events.

Subwoofer: A component of a loudspeaker system that is designed to reproduce very low bass frequencies.

Suitcasing: When a company tries to sell its product or service on the show floor without the permission or consent of the event's management.

Suite: A class of accommodations that is larger than a typical hotel room and usually contains a separate sitting room and may contain other facilities.

Suite Hotel: A hotel whose entire inventory of sleeping rooms have separate bedroom, bathroom, living room or parlor areas, and possibly a kitchenette or other special features. Also called ALL SUITE HOTEL.

Superimposition: Technique of projecting two visual images on a screen at the same time.

Supplemental Liability Coverage: In a car rental agreement, additional coverage for injury and damage claims by third parties beyond the amount provided automatically under the contract terms.

Supplier: Purveyor, provider, vendor, contractor offering facilities, products and/or services.

Support Staff: Part- or full-time personnel who provide services for tasks associated with programmes, events, or conventions.

Surcharge: Charge over and above established rates, such as an energy surcharge.

Surname: Name by which all immediate family members are known. Women usually (but not always) adopt their husband's surname upon marriage. Also called LAST NAME, FAMILY NAME. Compare with GIVEN NAME.

Suspended Elements: An attachment of devices to the frame work of an exhibition hall.

Switchboard: A combination of switches, dimmer plates and fuses for controlling light. See DIMMER BOARD.

Switcher: **1)** Engineer (technical director) who is switching from camera to camera. **2)** Panel with rows of buttons that allows switching from one camera or sound source to another.

Syndicate Room: See BREAK-OUT ROOM.

Symposium: A meeting of a number of experts in a particular field, at which papers are presented and discussed by specialists on particular subjects with a view to making recommendations concerning the problems under discussion.

Synchronization: (Sync) Sound and picture recorded or played back at the same time.

T-3 Line: Transmitting data at speeds of up to 44.184 Mbps, is faster than a T-1 line, allowing performance of more tasks simultaneously at a greater speed.

T-Shape Set-Up: Series of tables set up in the shape of the block T with chairs set all around except at the head table.

Table Tent: A folded sign placed on a table used to identify speakers, list menus or provide other information.

Table-Top Display/Exhibit: Small portable display that can be set up on top of a table.

Tare Weight: The weight of a container and/or packing materials deducted from the total weight to determine the weight of the contents or load. See ACTUAL WEIGHT, GROSS WEIGHT.

Target Date: A date set by event management and/or general service contractor for the arrival of freight at a trade event. Usually shipments received before or after this date are assessed a penalty charge.

Target Language: Language into which a speech or document is translated or interpreted.

Tariff: 1) A schedule of duties imposed by a government on imported and exported goods. **2)** Published list of fares or rates and conditions of service from a supplier.

Tax & Tip (T&T)**:** Addition of taxes and gratuities to a price when not included, designated by + +.

Tax Exempt Certificate: Document needed from customer to verify tax exemption status in the locale where the event is held.

Team of Interpreters: A group of people responsible for interpreting simultaneously by utilizing equipment.

Tear Down: Dismantle.

Teaser: Promotional piece designed to build interest in an event.

Tech Check: Review of all technical aspects of the production.

Technical Director: Person who calls cues from the control room.

Technical Meeting: An event with attendees who are involved in research, applied sciences, engineering or technology or are suppliers to them.

Technical Rehearsal: Run-through of technical aspects of an event such as lighting, sound, special effects, etc.

Technical Writer: Someone hired by a speaker to prepare scripts, workbooks, audios, videos, or articles on contract.

Technician: Expert in particular craft or technique usually in relation to audiovisual, mechanical or electrical equipment or appliances.

Teleconference: Type of meeting which brings together three or more people in two or more locations through telecommunications.

Teleprompter : Electronic device which allows display of script for speaker to read during presentation. May be referred to by brand names TelePrompTer ® (US), and Autocue (UK).

Temporary Import: Exhibition material whose temporary import status exempts payment of duties and taxes on arrival.

Temporary Import Bond: The surety covering articles imported into a country on a temporary basis, generally in lieu of paying import duties and/or taxes. The fee for the bond is non-refundable in most cases.

Tentative Agenda: A preliminary agenda for a programme, that is subject to change. See also PRELIMINARY Programme.

Tentative Hold: A space temporarily held by a facility or venue for a specific date pending a definite booking. There are no consequences for cancellation. See OPTION.

Theatre: Facility with fixed seats usually on a sloped floor with site lines focused on a permanent state. Typically a stage box is located behind the proscenium which contains the performance area and the fly loft.

Theatre Semicircular Set-Up: Seating arrangement in which seats are in semicircular rows facing the stage area, no tables.

Theatre Set-Up: Seating arrangement in which seats are in rows facing the stage area, no tables. See AUDITORIUM SET-UP.

Theme Break: A break during formal programme sessions with special food and beverages pertaining to a theme and often including decorations, costumes, and entertainment.

Theme Party: Event at which all foods, beverages, decorations, and entertainment relate to a single theme.

Think Tank: A group of specialists organised by a business enterprise, governmental body and commissions to undertake intensive study and research into specified problems.

Third Party Planner: An outsourced meeting or event planner.

Three Sheet: Bed made with a third sheet on top of the blanket. Also called TRIPLE SHEET.

Ticket Exchange: Banquet-control procedure whereby guests exchange an event coupon from their registration packet for an actual event ticket and seat assignment. Increases control. Also tends to reduce the number of no shows to provide more accurate guarantees.

Tiered: 1) One or more rows arranged above each other. **2)** Price levels of guest room rates.

Time Delay: Length of time between the production of live sound and when it is actually heard.

Time Lines: Includes each task to be accomplished and is the core of the programme plan.

Timecode: The sequential numbers assigned to each frame of video or film representing the passage of time in hours, minutes, seconds, and even tenths of seconds. Time codes are used for cataloging purposes and during editing.

Tour Broker: An individual licensed and bonded by the Interstate Commerce Commission to operate motor coach tours in the US and, in some cases, Canada. See TOUR OPERATOR.

Tour Escort: A person, usually employed or subcontracted (or independently contracted) by a DESTINATION MANAGEMENT COMPANY, who accompanies a tour from departure to return, as a guide. 2) A person who performs such functions only at the destination.

Tour Operator: A person or company that creates and/or markets inclusive tours and/or subcontracts their performance. Most tour operators sell through travel agents and/or directly to clients.

Tour Package: 1) Prearranged combination of elements such as air, hotel, sightseeing and social events packaged together and sold as an all-inclusive package price, not sold by component parts. **2)** To package, meaning to combine elements as above into an all-inclusive package product sold as such at a package price. See PACKAGE.

Tower: Structure to which lighting instruments are attached.

Trade Association: Group of persons or businesses in a particular trade or industry. Generally these organisations have a membership body and may be tax exempt.

Trade Fair: See EXHIBITION.

Trade Show: An exhibition of products and/or services held for members of a common or related industry. Not open to the general public. See EXHIBITION. Compare with GATE SHOW, PUBLIC SHOW, CONSUMER SHOW.

Trade-Out: A type of barter. The exchange of goods and services instead of using money.

Traffic Density: A way of calculating exhibition hall traffic. Typically expressed as the number of attendees for 100 square feet of exhibits.

Traffic Flow: 1) Movement of people through an area. **2)** A supposed or directed path that attendees will take through an exhibition.

Transfer: 1) Process of moving equipment and/or people from one point to another. **2)** Transportation between terminals and hotels. **3)** To copy a picture or sound that is transmitted by one recorder to another, or to make a tape or digital copy from film.

Transformative Learning: Learning that occurs during the second half of life which is directed at attaining a new consciousness and self-understanding.

Transient: Short term hotel guests who are not part of a group booking.

Transient Occupancy Tax (TOT): Tax placed on hotel/motel room rentals. Generally part of this revenue is used to market the destination and may be used for financing the operation of convention facilities. Also called BED TAX, ROOM TAX.

Transit: Passenger changing planes without going through security and/or customs.

Transit and Exhibition Insurance: The insurance that covers loss or damage caused deliberately or accidentally by third parties during loading, unloading, transshipment, transport, and exhibition.

Transit Visa: Visa allowing holder to stop over in a country to make a travel connection or for a brief visit.

Trapping: Method of consolidating shipments. Usually defines function of a LESS THAN TRUCKLOAD (LTL) trucker grouping freight for shipment to a particular show.

Trim Props: Props arranged to decorate the set. Also called SET DRESSING.

Triple Sheet: Bed made with a third sheet on top of the blanket. Also called THREE SHEET.

Tripod Screen: Portable projection screen (usually not larger than 10-12 feet) with three folding legs and a pull-up surface supported by a rod on the back.

Truck Loaders: Union labour specifically responsible for unloading equipment.

Truckload Rates: Truckload rates apply where the tariff shows a truckload minimum weight. Charges will be at the truckload minimum weight unless weight is higher.

Truss: 1) A frame to carry the room of a tent. **2)** A structure of steel bars used to suspend lighting or other technical equipment over a stage. **3)** To tie or bind something tightly.

Tube Lights: A string of small, low voltage lights contained in a clear or transparent coloured plastic tube, generally wired to be run by a three- or four-circuit sequencer (controller); used as a highlighter around signs, stages, or entrances. They can be bent and mounted on pegboard or other surfaces to form lighted words.

Turn-Around Time: 1) The time it takes to return to your original point of departure during a continuous move. **2)** Time it takes to breakdown and reset a room.

Turn-Down Service: Early evening service in which bed linens are "turned down", preparing the bed for use. May also include placing a confection, such as a chocolate or mint, on the pillow.

Turnaround: An action required to break down and reset a room.

Turnkey Exhibit: A system whereby the exhibit manager turns responsibility of the display over to an exhibit house. In essence, the exhibitor simply 'turns the key' upon arrival at the event and opens the booth/stand.

TV Monitor: A type of screen used to show a video image, which has denser pixels (for a sharper image) than a normal television screen.

Tweeter: Loudspeaker designed to reproduce high frequencies only. Tweeters are typically use at frequencies beyond the centre of the audio spectrum which, if placed on a logarithmic scale like a piano keyboard, would be about 630 Hz. Also known as a treble speaker.

Two-Tiered Set-Up: A seating arrangement with a row of seats on low risers around a BOARDROOM SET-UP. A very space-intensive set-up.

U-Shape Set-Up: Series of tables set up in the shape of the letter U with chairs set around one or both sides.

U.S. Travel Association (USTA): USTA is a member of the Convention Industry Council.

UL 2305: Standard for safety for exhibition display units.

Ultraviolet Lamp: A black light used to make phosphorescent and fluorescent paints glow in the dark.

Unconference: This is a participant-led event. The agenda is typically created by the attendees on arrival and includes open discussions rather than formal presentations.

Underground Hospitality Suite: Hospitality suite that is not hosted by an official sponsoring organisation (liability risk).

Underliner: Plate used under bowl, glass, condiments, and so forth. See BASE PLATE.

Unexpected Departure: A guest who checks out of a housing facility (hotel, motel, etc.) one or more days earlier than his or her scheduled departure date. Also called under-stay, EARLY-OUT. Compare with OVERSTAY.

Union Call: 1) The number of union members hired to work for an event. **2)** Additional servers obtained from a labour source shared by several hotels. **3)** The minimum number of hours for which a union labourer must be paid, regardless of actual hours worked.

Union Jurisdiction: The limits or territory within which control may be exercised by a union may be of at least two kinds. One has to do with geographical limits; the other with trade or craft activity.

Union Shop: A unionized business in which the employer by agreement is free to hire nonmembers as well as members of the union. Newly-hired employees are required, as a condition of employment, to join the union within a specified time after employment. All employees must maintain good standing in the union as a condition of employment.

Uniserve Property: A hotel property in which the convention services manager (CSM) handles all aspects of the event, including catering.

Up-Linking: The sending of video signals via microwave to an existing satellite for transmission to selected sites or anyone capable of satellite reception for that signal; used for teleconferencing or broad distribution of a message on a national or international basis.

Uplink: The station used to transmit signals from Earth to a satellite (videoconferencing).

Upstage: Part of the stage farthest from the audience or camera.

Use Day: Term used as a base unit in calculating occupancies. Various facilities have developed different definitions; one of the most common is use of all or part of a facility by one client or tenant for all or part of one day for any purpose; includes event, move-in, move-out and hiatus days.

V-Shape Set-Up: Seating arrangement in which chairs or tables and chairs are arranged in rows slanted in a V shape and separated by a centre aisle. They face the head table or speaker. See HERRINGBONE SET-UP. See also CHEVRON SET-UP.

Valance: 1) A trim or finish curtain, usually 12" deep with scalloped edge, used to give a tent a finished appearance. **2)** A short overhead, decorative border normally used as a light baffle or screen.

Validated Export License: A document issued by the U.S. Government authorizing the export of commodities for which written export authorization is required by law.

Value Added Tax (VAT)**:** A tax that is added to a product at each step of the manufacturing and marketing process reflecting value which has been added to the product by processing.

Value Season: See LOW SEASON.

Variable Costs or Expenses: Costs that vary according to the number of attendees, such as food and beverage or printed materials.

Varietal Wine: Wines made mainly from one variety of grape. Such wines have the characteristics of the primary grape used. Popular varietals are: Cabernet Sauvignon, Chardonnay, Chenin Blanc, Gewurztraminer, Pinot Noir, Sauvignon Blanc and Zinfandel.

VAT: See VALUE ADDED TAX

Vegan: A person who does not eat or use animal products or by-products for food, clothing, cosmetic or other purposes.

Vegetarian: A person who does not eat meat, poultry, fish or shellfish. Ovo-vegetarian: A person who does not eat meat, poultry, fish, or shellfish, but does consume eggs. Lacto-ovo vegetarian: A person who does not eat meat, poultry, fish, or shellfish, but does consume dairy products and eggs.

Venue: 1) Site or destination of meeting, event or show **2)** Location of performance such as hall, ballroom, auditorium, etc.

Verbatim Report: A full and exact word-for-word transcript, in writing, of all speeches, debates or discussions.

Vertical Show: An exhibition at which the products or services being displayed represent one element of an industry or profession. See EXHIBITION.

Vertical Union: Union with jurisdiction over all occupations, skilled and unskilled, in an entire industry.

Very Important Person (VIP)**:** Person who has a special function at the event (speaker, dignitary, etc.) and should be treated with special care and attention.

Video Character Generator: A computer-assisted device used to generate and create letters, numbers and symbols electronically. In simple terms, it is a video image that can also be used to recap key points made by a speaker or supply basic information such as final credits.

Video Enhancement: The enlargement of a video image from the size of a typical consumer television screen to dimensions for large projection screens. Used when attempting to present a larger-than-life image to an audience. See VIDEO MAGNIFICATION.

Video Formats: Type and size of the recording format in which a video presentation is recorded or played back. These include VHS (the most common), Beta, U-Matic, 1 inch, ¾ inch and ½ inch.

Video Magnification: See IMAGE MAGNIFICATION. See also VIDEO ENHANCEMENT.

Videoconference: A meeting between two or more people or groups across a distance, including video, audio, and potentially other data, utilizing telecommunications or communications satellites for transmission of the signal. See TELECONFERENCE.

Videowall: Array of video screens in a rectangular fashion on which images may be displayed individually on each screen or portions of the same image may be displayed in an enlarged format involving the whole or part of the array.

Vintage: Wine made from a grape harvest of a specific year. A vintage wine is made using 95 percent of those grapes. Wines made from grapes harvested from several years are called nonvintage.

Virtual Conferencing: Any meeting where people at two or more distant locations are linked using video, audio and data for two-way communication via satellite communications or the Internet. Each party sees and hears the other through a TV screen or computer monitor and audio speakers.

Virtual Tour: Any tour where people at two or more distant locations are linked using video, audio and data for communications. Each party sees and hears the tour through a TV screen or computer monitor and audio speakers.

Virtual Trade Show: Exhibit of products or services that can be viewed over the internet.

Visa: Permit, recorded in a passport, to enter a country for a specific purpose and period of time.

Visqueen: A clear plastic sheeting used to protect booth carpeting during move-in and set-up of a trade show. Technically a brand name, it is applied generically in common usage.

Voice Over: Announcement or other narrative copy which is "voiced" over the top of film, video or musical programming.

Voicing: Equalization of sounds produced by a system such as a piano or a loudspeaker so that the audio spectrum is produced evenly with all notes or frequencies at the same volume.

Waiter Parade: White gloved servers circle the room, usually with flaming dishes, before placing the food on the tables with a flourish.

Waiver of Subrogation: 1) A release of rights to substitute one party for another party. **2)** The release of an insurance company right to succeed to the insured's rights to sue for damages against the tortfeasor, after the insurance company pays an insured's claim of loss due to another's tort.

Walk: Guest holding confirmed sleeping room reservation is denied accommodations, typically due to a lack of available rooms, at the hotel where the reservation is held upon their arrival, and is relocated to another hotel.

Walk Away Clause: See CANCELLATION CLAUSE.

Walk-In: 1) Guest requesting accommodations without a prior reservation. **2)** Event attendee who has not pre-registered.

Walk-In/Out Music: Music accompanying arriving and exiting guests at an event (processional, recessional).

Walk-On: Music played while a new presenter arrives on stage.

Walk-Through: 1) Review of event details. **2)** Site inspection. **3)** Inspection of function room prior to function. **4)** Inspection of exhibit floor prior to opening of the event.

Wash: The difference between number of reservations at cut-off date and the number of final reservations at the end of an event. Can be positive or negative and be expressed as a number or percentage. See also CANCELLATION/NO-SHOW PERCENTAGE.

Wash Light: Coloured light that softly illuminates an area.

Waybill: A non-negotiable instrument of transport that serves as a receipt for the shipper, indicating that the carrier has accepted the goods listed therein and obligates itself to carry the consignment to the destination according to specified conditions. See also BILL OF LADING, INLAND BILL OF LADING, THROUGH BILL OF LADING.

Webcast: An event that broadcasts the audio and/or video portion of a keynote presentation or other educational sessions over the Web in real-time or on-demand.

Webconferencing: Web browser-based videoconferencing.

Well Brand: An economomical choice of brands of wine or distilled spirits above the house brand.

Wharfage: A charge assessed by a pier or dock owner for handling incoming or outgoing cargo.

Whispered Interpretation: Interpretation by an interpreter in a low voice to the audience usually while sitting next to the interpreter. See CONSECUTIVE INTERPRETATION, INTERPRETATION IN RELAY, SIMULTANEOUS INTERPRETATION, WIRELESS INFRARED INTERPRETING SYSTEM.

White Noise: Random noise whose various frequency components all share the same energy density characteristics, producing the same voltage at any particular discrete frequency over a period of time. This causes a frequency response trend that rises the same number of decibels as the percentage of frequency increase.

White Tie: Formal dress requiring white tie and tails for men and formal evening dress for women. See BLACK TIE.

Whiteboarding: A feature of videoconferencing systems which allows the placement of shared documents on an on-screen shared space or "whiteboard." Participants can edit and mark up the document just as on a physical whiteboard.

Windscreen: Porous cover for microphones to block unwanted sounds.

Wings: Off-stage area out of audience sight lines.

Wireless Access Point (WAP): A device that allows a connection to a wired network from a wireless device.

Wireless Infrared Interpreting System: An interpreting system operated by radio waves and hence without wire or cable connections to audience headsets. See CONSECUTIVE INTERPRETATION, INTERPRETATION IN RELAY, SIMULTANEOUS INTERPRETATION, WHISPERED INTERPRETATION.

Work Rules: Jurisdictional regulations which govern union craftsperson's working arrangement, include what work exhibitor may perform, when overtime begins, etc.

Workshop: 1) Meeting of several persons for intensive discussion. The workshop concept has been developed to compensate for diverging views in a particular discipline or on a particular subject. 2) Informal and public session of free discussion organised to take place between formal plenary sessions or commissions of a congress or of a conference, either on a subject chosen by the participants themselves or else on a special problem suggested by the organisers. 3) Training session in which participants, often through exercises, develop skills and knowledge in a given field.

Yield Management: A financial management method of pricing and capacity control that yields maximum profit. History, occupancy data, and competition are among the considerations used in this method.

Zero-Based Budgeting: The process of building a budget without benefit of a previous year's budget.

British-English Style Sheet

For use with the CIC Industry Glossary.

This Style Sheet is divided into three sections:

I.   Spelling, Grammar, and Style

II.   General Usage

III. Industry-Specific Applications

NOTE: *In all sections, the American word or spelling is listed in the leftmost column, with the British equivalent to the right.*

Different Spelling of Certain Word Groups

American Spelling	British Spelling	Examples of British Spellings
-er	-re	*centre, theatre*
-ize	-ise	*criticise, agonise, utilise, organise*
-or group	-our	*colour, favour, honour, labour*
e	-ce	*defence, pretence; licence* and *practice* are nouns but *license* and *practise* are preferred as verbs
-tion	-xion	*connexion, inflexion,* but *confection* and inspection
The British double the consonants of certain conjugated and derived word forms.		Conjugated forms: *travelled, travelling* Derived forms: *traveller, jeweller*
The British maintain the diphthongs *ae* or *oe* in words of Greek derivation, while Americans usually drop the *a* or *o*.		*aetiology, anaesthesia, anaemia, oedema, oenology, oesophagus*

Prepositions (in alphabetical order by preposition)

American Use	British Use	Examples/Notes
mad *about*/crazy *about*	mad *on*/crazy *on*	
nervous *about* (doing something)	nervous *of*	
something *along* those lines	something *on* those lines	
at auction	*by* auction	
liability *for*	liability *to*	e.g. income tax, special charges, etc.
sit *for* (pose)	sit *to*	
different *from*	different *to*	
a study *in*	a study *of*	applies where *study* is used to mean "striking example"
membership *in*	membership *of*	In both contexts, one is a member *of*, rather than a member *in*, an organisation.
frontage *on*	frontage *to*	
located *on* a street	located *in* a street	Although in Britain, one would still refer to being located *on* a road.
on form	*in* form	
dry *out*	dry *off*	
advantage *over*	advantage *of*	
increase *over*	increase *on*	
other *than*	other *to*	(infrequent)
thru	through	The colloquial spelling of *through* as *thru* does not exist Britain as it does in America.
cater *to*	cater *for*	(in the sense of *pander to*)
visit *to* London	visit *of* London	
write (someone)	write *to* (someone)	
under the circumstances	*in* the circumstances	
audience *with* (someone)	audience *of* (someone)	
chat *with*	chat *to*	
infatuated *with*	infatuated *by*	

Numbers

Meaning of a Billion

- In Britain, prior to 1974, a billion meant a million million, not a thousand million as in the U.S. In 1974, a billion was changed to refer to a thousand million in Britain.

- In most of continental Europe, words sounding similar to a billion are used to signify a million million.

- To avoid misunderstanding, it may be better to use these phrases instead of billion.

Decimal Points

- On the continent decimal points are represented by a comma (,) instead of a period (.), but only when written manually (not on the computer):

- e.g. 3,33 instead of 3.33

Emergency Services

- In Britain, dial 999 (or the European Union emergency number, 112). In the United States and Canada, dial 911.

Numerical Expressions

- double digits (U.S.) are referred to as double figures (UK), although this use is mostly informal

- twice/two times or three times something (U.S.) would be double or treble it (UK)

Money

- American money consists of Dollars ($) and Cents (¢)

- British money consists of Pounds (£) and Pence (p; pronounced "pee")

- The Euro (€) is used in Austria, Belgium, Cyprus, Estonia, Finland, France, Germany, Greece, Ireland, Italy, Latvia, Lithuania, Luxembourg, Malta, the Netherlands, Portugal, Slovakia, Slovenia, and Spain.

Time and Dates

Time of Day

- In Britain, a period rather than a colon is used between hour and minutes

- e.g. 2.30 instead of 2:30

Military time, or the 24 hour clock as it is referred to in Britain, is widely used in the UK and Europe.

- e.g. 13:30 instead of 1:30pm

Time is told differently:

- e.g. half ten (UK) instead of ten thirty (U.S.); quarter past ten (UK) instead of quarter after ten or ten fifteen (U.S.); quarter to ten (UK) instead of quarter of ten (U.S.)

Expressions of time:

- In Britain, momentarily means that something will only happen for an instant, rather than its U.S. meaning of something that will happen very soon.

- counter-clockwise (U.S.) is instead anti-clockwise (UK)

- two weeks (U.S.) is referred to as a fortnight (UK)

Date Format:

- dd/mm/yy (UK) versus mm/dd/yy (U.S.)

- e.g. May 10, 2020 would be written 10/5/20 (UK) instead of 5/10/20 (U.S.)

Measurements

1.20 gallons (approx.)	1 gallon
1.20 quarts (approx.)	1 quart
14 pounds	1 stone
ton (2,000 lbs.)	ton (2,240 lbs.)

Hospitality and Event Management

American Use	British Use	Examples/Notes
bed and breakfast (B&B)	bed and breakfast (B&B)	In the UK, B&Bs are usually the most affordable accommodation available, and are not as "done up" as those in America.
custom	bespoke	Something is bespoke if it's created especially for someone: a computer program may be bespoke for a client, or a travel agent may offer a bespoke holiday in which an itinerary is created around the client's exact requirements.
information	enquiries	This applies to signage, e.g. offices/desks that in the U.S. would be called 'Information' would in the UK be labeled "Enquiries". It also applies to the telephone directory function (see TELEPHONE TERMS).
party	do	e.g. a leaving party would be a "leaving do"
semiannual; semiannually	half-yearly	
initiation fee	entrance fee	fee paid upon joining a club
run for office	stand for election	
table	table	In the UK, to table a motion means it is brought to the table or suggested for consideration, whereas in the U.S. it would mean to leave the motion for a later date. In the U.S., the British meaning of "table" would translate as "submit for discussion."
over	PTO	to indicate a form should be turned over. PTO is an abbreviation for "please turn over".
to check	to tick	in reference to boxes on a form
handwriting (noun)	hand	
engrave	dye stamp	
tent	marquee	e.g. A large tent one would rent to hold a wedding reception.
gap	gangway	e.g. the space between a row of seats, where one can walk
thumbtack	drawing pin, push-pin	
copier, Xerox machine	photocopier	
adhesive tape, Scotch tape	sticky tape, Sellotape	
program	programme	In the UK, program is used to refer to computer programs.
site inspection	show around	
room rental	room hire	

act of God	*force majeure*	
general session	plenary	
classroom	schoolroom	
breakout rooms	syndicate rooms	
crescent rounds	cabaret	
theater	theatre, concert	
note pads	block notes	
tentative hold	first option	
waitlisted	second option	
vacation	holiday	Also in the UK, there are several bank holidays – so called because the banks close on these days, as do most businesses – which are like public holidays in America.
last name	family name	
Monday through Friday (inclusive)	Monday to Friday	
program	programme	In the UK, program is used to refer to computer programs.

Mail Terms

American Term	British Term	Examples/Notes
Styrofoam	polystyrene	Styrofoam is a brand name commonly used to refer to polystyrene in the U.S.
mail	post	
package	parcel	
shipping & handling	postage (posting) & packing	
overseas shipping	export carriage	
mail order buying	postal shopping	
postpaid	post-free	
general delivery	poste restante	
zip code	post code	
mailbox	post box, letter box	

Telephone Terms

American Term	British Term	Examples/Notes
to call	to ring	
busy (adj.)	engaged	One would say a line is engaged in the UK rather than busy. Likewise, if someone is talking on the telephone, instead of saying, "He's busy," one would say, "He's engaged." Engaged is also applied to someone who is in conference or in a meeting.
pound sign	hash	In the UK, pound sign denotes the monetary symbol £, not a telephone key.
cellular (cell) phone	mobile (phone)	
call collect	reverse the charges	
information, directory assistance	directory enquiries	
private line	exclusive line	
phone booth	kiosk, telephone box	Kiosk in the UK also refers to a newsstand.
white pages	telephone directory	Yellow pages is used in both the UK and U.S.
unlisted	ex-directory	Referring to telephone numbers.

Financial, Banking and Legal Terms

American Term	British Term	Examples/Notes
dollar sign ($)	pound sign (£)	
bill	note	Referring to paper money
value added tax or sales tax	VAT	The main difference in the UK is that VAT is included in the price of goods, not added at the till.
cash machine	till	
employees, personnel	staff	In the UK, use "staff only" on business signage
short-handed	short-staffed	
employment agency	staff bureau, staff agency	
résumé	CV (curriculum vitae)	
pay check	pay packet	
wage control	wage restraint	
payroll	wages sheet	
pay raise	pay rise	
check	cheque	
schedule of charges	tariff	In the UK, tariff can be used alone to mean "hotel charges" or "restaurant charges".
teller (in banks)	cashier	
ATM	cashpoint (machine)	
bank loan	overdraft	In the UK, overdraft refers to a loan arranged in advance, and does not hold any of the implications of an inadvertent overdraft, as does the American usage.
electronic funds transfer	direct debit, standing order	
uncollected funds	effects not cleared	
insufficient funds	refer to drawer	
stockholder	shareholder	
stocks (in a company)	shares	
Annual Meeting of Stockholders, Special Meeting of Stockholders	Annual General Meeting (AGM), Meeting of the Shareholders	
(insurance) coverage	cover	
insurance deductible	excess	
insurances arranged	insurances	
solicitor	refers specifically to an attorney	
attorney, lawyer	barrister, solicitor	

Buildings and Accommodation

American Term	British Term	Examples/Notes
floor (of a building)	storey	
first floor +	ground floor, then 1st floor, then 2nd, etc.	
elevator	lift	
lobby, front desk	reception	
entrance (signage)	entry	In the UK entrance is also used.
exit (signage)	way out	
bathroom, restroom	toilet, WC (water closet)	
living room	lounge, drawing room, sitting room	In the UK, living room is also used.
sign	board	e.g. notice board
apartment	flat	
dormitory	hall of residence	
garbage, trash	rubbish	
garbage can/trash can	(rubbish) bin (inside the house), dustbin if outside the house	
fire department	fire brigade	
driveway	drive	
sidewalk	pavement	
yard	garden	
swinging door	swing door	
sunken garden	sunk garden	
baseboard	skirting board	
(walk-in) closet	(walk-in) wardrobe	
wall-to-wall (carpet)	edge-to-edge (carpet)	
comforter (bed sheet)	duvet	

Audiovisual

American Term	British Term
extension cord/lead	flex
electric socket	power point
commercial	advert, ad, advertisement
TV show	TV programme
teleprompter	autocue
LCD projector	pointer, projector

Transport

American Term	British Term
divided highway, freeway	dual carriageway, motorway
detour	diversion
gas	gas (cooking, heating) petrol (cars)
gas station	petrol station
traffic circle	roundabout
rental car	hire car
tire	tyre (tire retains its other meaning of "to be worn out")
hood (of a car)	bonnet
trunk (of a car)	boot
tractor trailer; truck driver	lorry; lorry driver
bus (long distance, e.g. Greyhound)	coach (bus refers to short, pay as you enter trips)
bus terminal	bus station
taxi	cab
parking lot	car park (normally uncovered)
parking garage with several levels	multi-story car park
airplane	aeroplane
roundtrip (ticket)	return (ticket)
coach (e.g. class on an airplane)	economy
railroad	railway
stop	call e.g. A train from Washington, D.C. to Boston might call (not stop) at NYC.

Food and Beverage

American Term	British Term
check (noun)	bill
cafeteria	canteen
flatware, silverware	cutlery
napkin	serviette
"to go"	"take away"
bartender	barmaid/barman
proprietor (in England, of a pub)	landlady/landlord
liquors	spirits
straight (alcohol)	neat
toothpick	cocktail stick

Apparel

American Term	British Term
pants	trousers (be careful, as pants refers to underwear in the UK)
tuxedo	dinner jacket
fancy dress	fancy dress implies a costume party in the UK
robe	dressing gown
sneakers	trainers
purse	handbag
wallet, pocket book	purse

Bandwidth and Networking Terms for Meeting & Event Professionals

ADSL Asymmetrical Digital Subscriber Line (ADSL). A SHARED ISP technology for delivering BANDWIDTH to a facility over phone wires. Provides speeds of up to 6 Mbps upload and download.

Asymmetric Bandwidth A term describing an Internet Service Provider (ISP) technology where the download and upload bandwidth are not equal.

Bandwidth The amount of data that can be transmitted (upload) or received (download) per second.

Bandwidth Management A collection of techniques used by the NETWORK SERVICE PROVIDER (NSP) to control the available BANDWDITH within a facility in order to ensure a consistent experience for all users.

Bandwidth Utilization Report A document issued by a NETWORK SERVICE PROVIDER (NSP) that shows the amount of BANDWIDTH used by a specific event (upload and download).

Best Effort (bandwidth) Data that may be delayed by a queuing system in order to allow PRIORITY data to pass first.

Dedicated Bandwidth A set amount of BANDWIDTH that is exclusively available to the end user or group.

Forced Home Page The web page a device is sent to after leaving a PORTAL PAGE. Typically used to promote the event, event sponsors, or facility services.

Hot Spot A physical area with a Wi-Fi signal.

Internet Service Provider Also ISP. A company that provides Internet connectivity. Typically the company only provides a single demarcation point (DEMARC) to the building and the connectivity within the building is then distributed by the Network Service Provider (NSP).

Latency The time (in milliseconds) it takes for Internet traffic to travel from a device to a server. Higher latency is an indication of a poorer quality network.

MiFi A portable personal HOT SPOT.

Network Service Provider Also NSP. A company that provides management and support of a wired and wireless network infrastructure within a facility. They are the primary contact for network services within a facility.

Portal Page The web page a device is redirect to when it first attempts to reach the Internet. Also known as a Splash Page, Landing Page, or Gateway Page. Typically used to prompt users to accept terms and conditions, enter an access code or other authentication.

Priority (bandwidth) A queuing system employed when there is network congestion to allow certain types of data to be prioritized.

Shared Bandwidth A set amount of BANDWIDTH distributed among all devices on a network.

Symmetric Bandwidth A term describing an Internet Service Provider (ISP) technology where the download and upload BANDWIDTH are equal.

VLAN Also, Virtual Local Area Network. A technique to segment or isolate a network into functional areas that may require specific BANDWIDTH or security attributes.

Wireless Density The theoretical number of wireless connections that can be supported at a specific BANDWIDTH within a specific space.

Wireless Access Point Also WAP. A device that allows a connection to a wired network from a wireless device.

APEX Workgroup on Bandwidth and High Speed Internet Access (HSIA)

MaryAnne Bobrow, *Bobrow Associates, Inc. CMP, CMM, CAE, CHE*

Charles Chan Massey, *SYNAXIS Meetings & Events, CMP*

Steve Enselein, *Hyatt Hotels The Americas*

Michael Owen, *EventGenuity*

John Pollard, *Sonic Foundry*

John Rissi, *PSAV (Workgroup Chair)*

Stuart Ruff, *The Risk and Insurance Management Society, Inc.,* CMP

Todd Walton, *MGM Resorts*

Appendix C

Reviewers: CMP Volunteers

Adelynne Waldie, CMP
Alesa G. McArthur, CMP
Amanda Friedrich (Pasek) CMP
Amanda Gourgue, CMP
Amanda McLeish, CMP
Amy Alder, CMP
Ann Buhl, CMP
Ann M. Luketic, CMP
Ann M. Luketic, CMP
Anne ONeill, CMP, CAE
Audra Franks, CMP
Barno Saturday, CMP
Bart Lasner, CMP
Beverly Johnson, CMP
Bonnie Kaye Stanley, CMP
Brian Crawford, CMP
Carol Y. Allerding, CMP
Carolyn Davis, CMP
Carrie Crabtree, CMP
Chanise Reese-Queen, CMP
Charisse Martinez, CMP
Cheryl Payne, CMP
Cheryll Decker, CMP, CMP
Christine Faiman, CMP
Christine Gutermuth, CMP
Colleen A. Rickenbacher, CMP
Colleen Schwoerke, CMP
Crystal Green, CMP
Crystal Page, CMP
Cybill Valentine, CMP
Cynthia P. Kane, CMP
D'Arcy Klingle, CMP
Darrieux Harvey, CMP
Davitta B. Ealy, CMP
Dawn Levesque, CMP
Deanna K. Griffith, CMP
DeAnna Moxley, CMP
Dena Rose, CMP, CMM
Denise Herrington, CMP
Devon Sloan, CMP
Dina O'Rourke, CMP
Elizabeth Brubaker, CMP

Elizabeth Lyons, CMP
Ellen Maiara, CMP
Erin Johnson, CMP, CMM
Erin Tench, CMP
Feborah M. Dixon, CMP
Felicia Watson, CMP
Frank Yang, CMP, CEM, PMP, MBA
Gail A Emery, CMP
Garet Turner, CMP
Genetta Vinson, CMP
H. Ramona Crayton, CMP
Heidi Hanrahan, CMP
Jamie Giacobbe, CMP
Jamilla Bell, CMP
Jamye Callery, CMP
Janet Graff, CMP
Jeffrey Cesari, CMP
Jennifer Clauson, CMP
Jennifer Haire, CMP
Jennifer Pilson, CMP
Jennifer Russo, CMP
Jennifer Spriggs, CMP
Jim Cacabelos, CMP
Jittaun Phillips, CMP, CMM
John Hawkins, CMP
Judy McClain, CMP
Kami Kinlaw, CMP
Karen Gonzales, CMP
Katie Whalen, CMP
Kay Bothwell, CMP
Kelly Kroh-Jones, CMP
Kelsey Soukup, CMP, CTA
Kevin M Kelly, CMP
Kim Fields, CMP
Kristen Keenan, CMP
Lauralee Shapiro, CMP
Lauren Mongeon, CMP
LaVasha Lobbins, CMP
Lee Avery, CMP
Leigh Bentley, CMP
Lesly Rehaut, CMP
Linda Muir, CMP

Lisa Boyd, CMP
Lisa Dyson, CMP
Lisa J. Mikita, CMP, CAE
Lisa Swett, CMP
Loretta Lowe, CMP
Lori Denning, CMP
LoriAnn K Harnish, CMP
Lourdes Kiki Gerardo, CMP
Lucinda Gooch, CMP
Maliek Van Laar, CMP
Marie Caci, MTA, CMP, CPCE, CSEP
Mariela McIlwraith, CMP, CMM, MBA
Marina Mitusova, CMP
Marlene Blas, MTA, CMP
Megan Lanning, CMP
Meredith Flanagan, CMP
Meredith Merritt, CMP
Michael D. Lynn, CMP
Michele Burnett, CMP
Michele Curlee, CMP
Milena Santoro, CMP
Ms Beri Kockaya, CMP
Nancy Short, CMP
Norah Webster, CMP
Rhonda Leach, CMP
Robert Chambers, CMP
Robin Hesselink, CMP
Sarah Harris Kreisler, CMP
Sarah Krebs, CMP
Scott Williamson, CMP
Shameka Allen, CMP
Sharon Collins, CMP
Sheris A Johnson, CMP
Stacie Ann Smith, CMP
Stacy Harvey, CMP
Susannah Winfield, CMP
Sydney Williams, CMP
Tami Gilbertson CMP
Tammy Benedict, CMP
Tammy Kicker, CMP
V. Scott Kerr, CMP
Veronica McKee, CMP

What's a CMP Preferred Provider?

CMP Preferred Providers are organisations that have formally registered with the Convention Industry Council (CIC) and are committed to providing education that aligns with one of the 10 domains included in the CMP International Standards (CMP-IS).

CMP Preferred Provider Program

Already have a CMP Portal Account?

After the event, the organiser will upload verified attendees If email matches – the education will appear on your portal account. You will receive an email notifying you that the event has been uploaded in your portal. All you have to do is enter the number of approved hours you participated in! No need to list every session separately!

Don't have a CMP Account?

CREATE ONE TODAY AT: myaccount.conventionindustry.org
Note: Your email on the CMP Portal must match the one you used to register for the education.

THE CMP- IS DOMAINS ARE: Strategic Planning, Project Management, Risk Management, Financial Management, Human Resources, Stakeholder Management, Meeting or Event Design, Site Management, Marketing and Professionalism.

Sign in to create your account and start tracking continuing education credits towards your CMP.

www.conventionindustry.org

Top Benefits For Attendees!

· Easily track your continuing education credits for the CMP program

· No need to show proof of attendance

· Sessions already aligned with one of the 10 domains of the CMP International (CMP-IS) or CMP Healthcare (CMP-HC) standards.

· Easily find CMP Preferred Provider education in one central location.

Top 4 career-enhancing benefits of earning (or maintaining) your CMP designation:

(1) **Industry Recognition**
(2) **Peer Acceptance**
(3) **Salary Enhancement**
(4) **Personal Achievement**